THE AMERICAS POETRY FESTIVAL OF NEW YORK 2014

MULTILINGUAL ANTHOLOGY

CARLOS AGUASACO & YRENE SANTOS (EDS.)

artepoética press

NEW YORK, 2014

Title: Multilingual Anthology: The Americas Poetry Festival of New York 2014
ISBN-10:1940075254
ISBN-13:978-1-940075-25-9

Design: © Ana Paola González
Cover & Image: © Jhon Aguasaco
Editor in Chief: Carlos Aguasaco
E-mail: carlos@artepoetica.com
Mail: 38-38 215 Place, Bayside, NY 11361, USA.

© Anthology: The Americas Poetry Festival of New York 2014, Carlos Aguasaco
& Yrene Santos (Eds.)
© Anthology: The Americas Poetry Festival of New York 2014, for this edition
Artepoética Press

THE
AMERICAS
POETRY FESTIVAL
OF NEW
YORK
2014

MULTILINGUAL ANTHOLOGY

WWW. POETRYNY.COM

Índice

On the Origin and Future of Poetry: Notes Towards an Investigation By Carlos Aguasaco[1]

What is the origin of poetry?

Poetry possibly preceded language, but a poem is an artifact that, like everything else in civilization, has a history. The first forms of acoustic communication may probably have emerged about 500,000 years ago. The first languages probably appeared about 50,000 years ago. The first poem in history must have been created around that same time. At first, words, like tools, were rudimentary and scarce. Migrations, new contexts and new needs of survival determined their process of sophistication and refinement. Living, or surviving, was not an easy task for the hairless hominids that we were that we are. Nevertheless, we have evidence of the creation of elaboration of complex cultural products (carvings, paintings, and tools) dating back 20,000 years. The Proto-Indo-European language existed some 6,000 years ago. Sumerian literature, the oldest we have material evidence of, emerged about 4,700 years ago.

Let us take a moment to analyze the conditions of production of the first poem in history. Is it possible to reconcile Charles Darwin's theory of evolution to the writing of poetry? Before attempting to answer this question it is worth discussing the neurological origins of language explained succinctly by Rodolfo R. Llinás (2001). Communication is not exclusive to humans. Animals manage to communicate by means of gestures, grunts and smells (among other things) information that is vital for their survival. A grunt can be an alarm signal, a gesture can convey submis-

---

1 Assistant Professor of Latin American Cultural Studies and Spanish in the Department of Interdisciplinary Studies at The City College of New York (CUNY). Born in Bogotá, Colombia (1975), he earned his Ph.D. at Stony Brook University (SUNY) and was awarded the prestigious W. Burghardt Turner Doctoral Fellowship by the State University of New York. He holds an M.A. in Spanish from The City College of New York (CUNY) and B.A. in Literature from the Universidad Nacional de Colombia. In 2010 Carlos won the India Catalina prize for best video in the art category at the Cartagena International Film Festival. As author and scholar, Professor Aguasaco has been invited to present his work in universities and cultural institutions of the US, Mexico, Cuba, Colombia, Dominican Republic, Puerto Rico, Honduras and Spain. His work has been included in numerous anthologies and featured in a variety of media outlets. He has coedited seven anthologies, authored three poetry collections and an academic study of Latin America's prime superhero El Chapulín Colorado. His main academic interests are: literary theory, contemporary poetry, transitional discourses, Latin American popular culture, and the residual ideologies of the Spanish Golden Age. He currently serves as director of the MA program in the Study of The Americas at CCNY.

sion to the alpha male in a wolf pack, and pheromones signal reproductive readiness (225-32). Every attempt of an organism to communicate with another requires the establishment of a community of meaning represented in a form of 'consensus.' The ability to imitate each other allows animals to develop a sense of familiarity and belonging to the pack. At some point, that capacity is transformed into both a need and a desire to communicate. Llinás states that acoustic imitation is privileged over imitation of gestures because the former allows the emitting animal to hear itself while transmitting the message. Visual systems of communication require stricter material conditions than acoustic media. In the theory of evolution, adaptation is the result of constant processes of trial and error. When sensing danger or feeling pain, an animal victim of a predator can, naturally, emit a cry of such intensity and volume that the attacker feels deterred and decides to leave (238). When the screech, cry of pain, is 'understood' as a signal of danger by the predator the first metaphor is born, perhaps by accident (238). The first metaphor was both an accidental and collective creation; it would be actually more appropriate to call it a proto-metaphor because although it already contains a logical base, it still lacks the expressive will of the emitter. The survival of the prey and its kind will depend, among other things, on its capacity to transform this circumstance into an effective symbolic instrument. In practice, the animal will no longer wait to feel pain to emit the 'noise' that can guarantee its survival. The cry of pain is known in neuroscience as a Fixed Action Pattern or reflex action. To construct a system of communication based on corporal expressions such as gestures and sounds, the brain must develop the capacity to control, i.e., at will, the systems of mechanical reaction that produce the Fixed Action Patterns. The gap between emission and interpretation that generates the momentary rupture in the link between action and reaction is the 'Big Bang' of linguistic systems and, therefore, of poetry. At the beginning of language, the trope, the simile and the metaphor are undistinguishable; poetry, like a zygote, is in an embryonic state. Greg Urban identifies the first non-instinctive signals as metasignals constructed on top of previous instinctive actions such as grunts and cries ("Metasignaling and Language Origin," 2002.) However, as the system grows and gains stability, instinctive reactions stop supplying the necessary tools for more complex forms of communication among the community and its succeeding generations. Meanwhile, natural selection permitted hominids to develop neocortal control over the laryngeal muscles (235) enabling them to produce and manipulate sounds. This development vastly exceeds any previous capacity to share linguistic tools and acquired information. The community now needs to develop new ways of conserving and sharing the linguistic developments that will represent a selective advantage over other species. The channel is the air and the recording device is memory. From this moment on, rhythm and repetition would share room with the Fixed Action Patterns. Memory, music, and poetry are now a single entity and they sustain each other reciprocally.

In the beginning, discourses, like other tools, were not specialized. At the time, discursive products had to 'serve' to address a variety of needs. For example, biblical texts, served as religious manuals, treatises on history, science, politics, law, pedagogy, art, etc. In fact, even today some nations take their religious books as the basis of their legal and political systems.[2] The best illustration is Sharia law, with one of its sources in the Koran, which was written in verse and continues to serve as spiritual guide and basis of legal doctrines. The writing of poems, then, did not emerge as an independent form or specialized form of communication. Poetry, in the most abstract sense, precedes the poem in the same way that spoken language precedes writing. It is also possible to say that poetry was the Siamese twin of history, philosophy, law, religion, science and mathematics. In practice, poetry maintained a social communication function for a long time. The emergence of new technologies such as writing began what I would call the process of emancipation and specialization of poetry. The poem, poetry's main instrument, thus began a slow process of liberation from legal and scientific functions to focus on its own self. Every poem is in itself a theory of poetry, a poetics.

In its origins, poetry serve man 'to grasp' knowledge relevant for survival. Poems were instruments of teaching and learning. How did the primitive poetic mechanism function? Probably, after the so-called 'Big Bang' of linguistic systems, a boom in experimentation and interpretation with acoustic signals began. The more 'effective' signals would become popular while others were short lived and disposed of. Poetry since the beginning has been the quest for new and richer meanings without abandoning past achievements. The most appropriate comparison would be the surgical method of bone lengthening in which a bone is artificially elongated using the natural process of osteogenesis. In a surgical intervention called corticotomy, the doctor provokes an artificial fracture in the bone and installs a system of screws that controls the distance between the two fractured sections. The gap must be big enough to allow for elongation, yet short enough to not impede it. At that moment, the fracture is a new 'event' for the bone but, once it has been repaired by process of osteogenesis, it becomes a support for new elongations. Language grows

---

2   This is the case of the many countries that base their laws on the Koran.

and extends itself thanks to 'fractures' in meaning that are basically the fundamental instruments of poetry. In 1844, Ralph Waldo Emerson correctly said "Every word was once a poem" (197). Poets were the makers of language or likewise, all makers of language have been poets. Following the same thought, Emerson said: "Poets made all the words and, therefore, language is the archive of history, and, if we must say it, a sort of tomb of the muses" (199). Languages are built with what he calls "fossil poetry" (199).

Writing, as a form of technology, breaks into the history of poetry with multiple effects. The onomastic model, Houston informs us (2004), explains the development of writing as an extension of preceding systems of numeric notation (236). From this perspective, writing would be a sibling of accounting and early forms of administration. Writing is one the material forms of power. Although the development of different writing systems requires an independent study, we must concentrate here on its influence in poetry. The oldest 'poetic' text we know of is "Hymn to the Death of Tammuz" dating back 2500 to 3000 years BC[3].

The equally ancient *Epic of Gilgamesh* is preserved on written tablets dating back to about 1200 BC. Writing was a new technology that took at least two millennia to become hegemonic. When texts like the *Epic of Gilgamesh* begin to be 'written' in stable materials such as clay tablets and stone, poetry entered the endless era of litigation, of debate, over meaning. The written text would eventually impose its authority over oral tradition. Paul Zumthor made a detailed study of the relationship between oral expression and literature in the middle ages. Beyond the process, how did writing affect poetry? One of its consequences was the materialization of poetry in an object, the poem. From that moment on, poems could be alienated, accumulated and possessed without requiring any intellectual effort of its 'owner.' Property could be extended and transferred beyond the lifespan of the 'proprietor.' The text could now be 'consumed' simultaneously in more than one place. The reproduction of written texts is the new alternative to memory. The poem, as object, enters more and more into private spaces. Nowadays, orality seems almost exclusively something from the past. However, we must remember that lyric poetry derives its name from the interpretations done in ancient Greece with a lyre or a flute by antique rhapsodes. The couple formed by Mimnermo and Nanno (7th century BC) has become part of history as an example or the prevalence of orality over writing.

---

3   It has recently been said that the poem "Dünyanın en eski aşk şiiri" also known as Istanbul #2461 (Its reference number in the Museum of Istanbul) is the oldest known love poem.

With the arrival of the printing press (1450) and the subsequent expansion of reading, poetry began to serve increasingly more the needs of the 'user' or 'consumer' and less and less the social group in general. To this end, the themes cease to be 'collective' and become the 'revelation' of particular realities. Lyric poetry becomes the poetry of the inner self while epic poetry becomes the sister of history and ruler of the external world. The personal becomes lyric and the social becomes epic. The epic evolves, Georg Lukács says into the modern novel.

We must remember that, as Asa Briggs and Peter Burke have correctly pointed out, as new communication channels and media have appeared, the old ones have not disappeared but coexist with them. Writing did not end orality but rather released it from its mnemotechnic function. The printing press did not end manuscripts but instead displaced them to the personal sphere while it took over the public arena. Photography did not end painting but released it from its mimetic function and allowed it to explore abstract universes. Film did not end the theater but instead established a symbiotic relation with it. Television did not mean the end of radio but its transformation into new forms of debate and analysis. In the same way, the internet will not eliminate any of its predecessors but will coexist with them in a reciprocal causality that will transform them all.

When transferring the same logic to poetry and its representative forms throughout history, we can see how epic poetry survives in certain forms of committed poetry. We also see that with the arrival of modernity (16th century), lyric poetry found the ideal form for representing the most intimate voice of the subject in the sonnet. Based on this, we can say that as long as the pronouns 'I' and 'You' exist, there will be forms lyric poetry; and as long as the pronouns 'We' and 'They' exis,t epic poetry will remain in different media and forms.

Has poetry had ontological crises?

Despite its permanence, we must recognize that throughout history poetry has had to confront ontological crises that provoked divisions, sub-specializations and changes. The first of these would be accepting that poetry was no longer the universal and almighty discourse of the 'Creator.' Some orthodox religions maintain this old idea in their prayers, rites and sacraments. However, the great majority of us read texts like the Bible not in a literal or scientific sense but as beautiful allegories with certain, although limited, historical truth. When Huidobro says that "The poet is a small God[4]" (*Espejo de Agua,* 1916), what he actually recognizes is that in

---

4   In the original "El poeta es un pequeño Dios."

our times poetry does not represent the voice of an endless and almighty giant but the shriek of a bunch of midgets. Huidobro's verse comforts the modern poet but it undoubtedly declares the extinction of the evangelist poet.

Martin Heidegger devoted two of his works on Hölderlin and Rilke to the study of poetry: "What Are Poets For?" and "Why Poets?" (1946.) According to this German philosopher, the poet is a creator that emerges in a world without 'god' or 'deities.' According to him, the poet is willing to take up the space abandoned by the 'gods.' However, an oppositional reading would bring to light that Heidegger is trying disguise and transfer his concept of "Being in the world" (*Dasein*) from the battleground to the territory of language, from the soldier's rifle to the poet's quill. Maybe without realizing it, Heidegger proposes a new teleology in which immortality can be achieved in the linguistic universe. His reading of poetry is an allegory of a world that has ceased to exist. -Where does his mistake lie?- When he presents Hölderlin and Rilke as 'precursors' who are unsurmountable by any poet of our era, Heidegger distorts the real figure of the poet that Huidobro clearly understood (*Poetry, Language...*142). In this case, it seems the German philosopher were in need of 'supermen' or 'supernatural beings' to keep his ideological construct from falling apart.

Why didn't he think about the power of women who can give life to another being inside their own bodies and then give it to the world to allow it to be itself? Why didn't he mention the mothers of Hölderlin and Rilke as their own 'precursors'? The first ontological crisis of poetry was inscribed within Descartes' discourse. The emergence of modern logic and its scientific counterparts made it inevitable.

Poetry came out of this crisis renovated and liberated from functions that are now assumed by archeology, law, history, biology, and medicine (among other sciences.) In modernity, poetry, like painting, was now free to explore the interior universe in which everything is language. From a heretotelic voice (a voice for all) it moves to an autotelic song in which the poem is a new and small totality. The *isms* of the 19th century and the 20th century avant-garde testify to this process.

The second ontological crisis (I say this to organize the discourse but it should not be taken in a linear sense) is the arrival of writing as a new technology. Writing frees poetry from its mnemotechnic function and yet it simultaneously loses the flexibility of orality. Poetry, in its oral phase, i.e., before writing, was a living organism with the capacity to accommodate itself to new contexts and the ability to articulate new contents each time it was transmitted orally from one person to another. The written poem is inflexible both in content and form. As a result of the new stability gained with writing, representative flexibility is transferred to hermeneutics. That is why today we have hundreds, perhaps thousands, of scholars attempting to 'understand' what Cesar Vallejo meant in his book *Trilce* (1922).

The third ontological crisis of poetry is the result of the consolidation of the market economy and capitalism. The concept of private property has invaded all spaces and spheres. The poem gains an exchange value represented in money or social acknowledgement. The so-called "Copy Rights" attach the poem to a historical subject with a legal ball and chain. I have discussed this topic in a previous article on the relationship between poetry and private property. In many cases, the historical author and his/her biography displace the content of the poem. In fact, not long ago, Peruvian author Alfredo Bryce Echenique received an award in the International Book Fair of Guadalajara amidst a scandal about alleged plagiarism on his part. This example, coming from narrative literature, reveals dramatic aspects of the role of literature as a cultural product with exchange value. Poetry contests, writing fellowships, and all sort of social events turn poems into merchandise in an ever-expanding market of cultural capital. In modernity, poetry was increasingly transformed into a battle ground of disputes and confrontation. The result has been an ethics based in an economic formation that favors inequality. This reality subjects lyric poetry to tension between representation of the subject's 'interiority' and its social subsistence. Modern hermeneutics approaches poetry by asking in strict order: Who? Why? In exchange for what? and What for?

The fourth ontological crisis of poetry is the questioning of its authenticity. Technological progress and the significant advance in literacy, have facilitated the emergence of authors from every possible social sphere. This is undoubtedly a significant achievement of our civilization. Anyone, and everyone can be a poet. Furthermore, many have begun to think that 'any' discourse whatsoever can be read and presented as a poem.

This reflection that stems from the visual arts was initiated by Marcel Duchamp with his theory of the so-called 'ready-made.' According to which, any object can be re-contextualized and re-signified as a work of art. Today, anyone can proclaim himself/ herself as a poet; in doing so, they claim their inalienable right to present any discourse as a poem. Therefore, there are those who present a grocery list as a poem, while others may present a chemical formula or a mathematical equation for the same purpose. Please do not confuse this discussion with the concept of the Poem-Object proposed by André Bretón or with the concretist poetry developed in Brazil. The current ontological crisis of poetry results from the overloading of all channels of communication with discourses 'declared' or 'presented' as poems that claim an exchange value in our cultural economy. Let us think, for a moment, what would happen if anyone could present herself / himself to an audience to play a musical instrument that he/she has never studied or learned to play. What would happen if all the spaces for music were invaded by characters claiming their right to play a musical instrument by pounding on it or scratching it? At this point, the snake bites its own tail because, as mentioned above, representative flexibility has now been displaced by hermeneutics. How will poetry emerge from this ontological crisis? There could be several outcomes, one would be that the new poet will is the reader and not the writer. In fact, I say this following Borges, each great poet is first a great reader.[5] Another possible outcome would be rise of an anonymous poetry movement looking for a valuation of artistic achievement based solely on the text itself and not on any extra-literary factors involved in its production.

What is the future of poetry?

I would like to finish this text with a brief reflection on the future of poetry as a result of its interaction with new technologies such as smart phones, social networks, internet, video games, etc. It is no secret that science and technology have reached a high level of development amidst a constant state of change. This sort of technical inertia makes new machines become obsolete every six months, forcing us to replace them with new 'upgraded' versions. How many of us change our cellphone at least once or twice a year? How many of us read at least some documents on computer screens? Time becomes shorter and shorter, not in a material sense but in our perception of it. Therefore, the stability of the Metaphor is at risk. The arrival and popularization of the automobile made many of the old metaphors related to the horse simply obsolete or degraded to second level. Airplanes had the same effect with respect to birds in poetry. The cell or 'mobile' phone transformed a spatial metaphor into one of constant displacement. The internet took away the perfume from many letters that are no longer written with quill and paper, with careful calligraphy and composition, but that on the contrary, have become more telegraphic, codified by teenagers using their thumbs in a frenetic race to respond immediately without reflecting on what they have written or read. To survive, poetry will have to resort to the fundamental metaphors mentioned by George Lakoff and Mark Johnson in their book *Metaphors We Live By* (1980). Another alternative would be for technology to provide an unlimited number of clarifying notes and hypertexts, as Severo Sarduy correctly envisioned. In conclusion, to survive, poetry will make reading precede writing and

---

5 The reader must be seen as decoder.

will also extend its presence throughout the entire process of communication. The future of poetry depends on the empowerment of the reader and the weakening of the link between poem and private property. In fact, the poetry of the future already exists but we have been incapable of reading it. It is a poetry that assumes the instability of metaphors and reacts against the preeminence of science as the hegemonic discourse on knowledge. The work of César Vallejo is the best example of this poetry of the future that demands empowerment and strengthening of the reader.

Finally, I invite the reader of this multilingual anthology to approach it in the light of these concepts and become involved in the current debate on the ontological definition of poetry. Today, more than ever before, poetry defines and constitutes humanity.

Bibliography

Aristotle. *On the Heavens*. Book II. Available at http://classics.mit.edu/ Aristotle/heavens.2.ii.html

Aguasaco, Carlos. "Escribir en Nueva York: una po-ética del sujeto en la crisis de la modernidad". La ventana portal informativo de Casa de las Américas, Julio 14 de   2011. http://laventana. casa.cult.cu/modules.php?name=News&file=article&sid=6286

Briggs, Asa, and Peter Burke. *A social history of the media: from Gutenberg to the   Internet*. Cambridge: Polity, 2002.

Emerson, Ralph Waldo. "The Poet." *Essays*. Pennsylvania: Electronic Classics Series Pennsylvania State University. 189-210. Available at http://www2.hn.psu.edu/faculty/jmanis/rw-emerson/essays_rwe.pdf

Flores, Ángel. *Aproximaciones a César Vallejo. Vols I y II*. New York: Las Americas, 1971.

Heidegger, Martín. "What Are Poets For?" *Poetry, Language and Thought*. Trad. Albert Hofdtadter. New York: Harper & Row, 1975. 91-142.

- - - . "Why Poets?" *Off the Beaten Track*. Julian Young & Kenneth Haynes Eds. and   Trads. Cambridge: Cambridge U Press, 2002. 200-241.

Henderson, Linda Dalrymple. *The Fourth Dimension and Non-Euclidean Geometry in Modern Art*. Princeton, NJ: Princeton UP, 1983.

Huidobro, Vicente. *Sus mejores poemas*. Biblioteca Zig-Zag. Los Grandes de la literatura chilena 1. 1a ed. Santiago de Chile: Zig-Zag, 1984.

Houston, Stephen D. "The Archaeology of Communication Technolo gies." *Annual Review of Anthropology*. 33 (2004): 223-250.

Ibérico, Mariano. "El Tiempo". *Aproximaciones a César Vallejo. Vols I*. New York: Las Americas, 1971.303-315

Kaku, Michio. *Hyperspace. A Scientific Odyssey Through Parallel Universes, Time Wraps And The 10th Dimension*. New York: Anchor Books, 1995.

Kramer, Samuel N. "The Oldest Literary Catalogue: A Sumerian List of Literary Compositions Compiled about 2000 B. C." *Bulletin of the American Schools of   Oriental Research*. 88 (Dec., 1942):10-19.

Lakoff, George, and Mark Johnson. *Metaphors we live by*. Chicago: Uni versity of Chicago Press, 2003.

Lukács, György. *The theory of the novel: a historico-philosophical essay on the forms of great epic literature*. London: Merlin Press, 1971.

Llinás, Rodolfo R. *I of the Vortex: From Neurons to Self*. 1st ed. Cambridge, Mass.: MIT Press, 2001.

Ortega, Julio. *La teoría poética de César Vallejo*. USA.: Del Sol Editores, 1986.

Riquer, Martín de, and José María Valverde. *Historia de la literatura universal: con textos antológicos y resúmenes argumentales. Vol 2. Literaturas medievales de transmisión oral*. Barcelona, España: Planeta, 1984.

Rodríguez, Juan Carlos. *Theory and history of ideological production: the f irst bourgeois literatures (the 16th century)*. Trans. Malcolm K Read. Monash Romance studies. 1st American ed. Newark [Del.]: University of Delaware Press, 2002.

Urban, Greg. "Metasignaling and Language Origin." American Anthro pologist, New Series. 104.1 (Mar., 2002): 233-246.

Vallejo, César. *Trilce*. Castalia didáctica. Madrid: Castalia, 1991.

- - - . *Poemas en prosa - Poemas humanos -España, aparta de mí este cáliz*. Madrid: Cátedra, 2000.

- - - . *Artículos y Crónicas Completos. Vols. I y II*. Lima: Pontificia Universi dad Católica del Perú, 2002.

Zumthor, Paul. *La letra y la voz de la literatura medieval*. Madrid: Cáte dra, 1989.

DIANA ARAUJO PEREIRA
[BRASIL]

Diana Araujo Pereira (Brazil, Río de Janeiro, 1972). Poet, translator and professor of Latin American Literature at Universidade Federal da Integração Latino-Americana in Foz do Iguaçu, Brazil. She has published two poetry collections: *Vientreadentro* (2006) &*Otras Palabras* (2008). She has also translated works by Antonio Cisneros, Pedro Granados, Juan Gelman, Omar Lara & Marco Lucchesi.

Diana Araujo Pereira (Brasil, Río de Janeiro, 1972). Poeta, traductora y profesora de literatura latinoamericana en la Universidade Federal da Integração Latino-Americana en Foz do Iguaçu. Ha publicado dos libros de poemas *Vientreadentro* (2006) &*Otras Palabras* (2008). También ha traducido textos de autores como Antonio Cisneros, Pedro Granados, Juan Gelman, Omar Lara & Marco Lucchesi.

XXVIII

No horizonte da espera
há barcos ancorados à terra
sonhando com despertar
na liberdade do mar.
No horizonte da espera
Há olhares suspensos
mensagens cifradas
fumegantes desejos
que aguardam o momento de desfazer os nós
e lançar-se ao tempo.

O horizonte, a linha de fronteira que une e separa,
a membrana de céu e terra que nos demarca,
guarda a arca da aliança,
guarda a promessa da alvorada
com suas luzes mescladas.

Este horizonte, que reconstrói passos
sobre velhos dilemas,
novos sendeiros sobre historias passadas.

Na linha que descansa sobre o horizonte
a esperança dorme no compasso da espera;
o tempo embala o futuro
que no final das contas alcança a alma.

Com o coração às cegas,
(olhos vendados, cegos de luminosidade)
cumpro com a respiração que a vida exala,
desenho cartografias estranhas,
retorno ao princípio do mundo.
A linha que aprisiona o horizonte é a mesma que nos obriga a andar.

XXVIII

En el horizonte de la espera
hay barcos anclados a tierra
soñando con despertar
en la libertad del mar.
En el horizonte de la espera
hay miradas colgadas
mensajes cifrados
humeantes deseos
que aguardan el momento de deshacer los nudos
y arrojarse al tiempo.

El horizonte, la línea de frontera que une y separa,
la membrana de cielo y tierra que nos enmarca,
guarda el arca de la alianza,
guarda la promesa del alba
con sus luces mezcladas.

El horizonte éste, que reconstruye pasos
sobre viejos dilemas,
nuevos senderos sobre historias pasadas.

En la línea que descansa sobre el horizonte
duerme la esperanza al compás de la espera;
acuna el tiempo el futuro
que al fin y al cabo nos atrapa el alma.

Con el corazón a tientas,
(ojos vendados, ciegos de luminosidad)
cumplo con la respiración que me exhala la vida,
dibujo cartografías extrañas,
retorno al principio del mundo.
La línea que aprisiona el horizonte es la misma que nos insta a andar.

XXVIII

In the awaiting horizon
there are boats anchored to the land
that dream of awaking
in the freedom of the sea.
In the awaiting horizon
there are hanging gazes
coded messages
smoky wishes
that wait for the moment to undo the knots
and throw themselves onto time.

The horizon, the line of the border that unites and divides,
the membrane of the sky and land that marks us,
keeps the ark of the alliance,
keeps the dawn's promise
with its mixed lights.

The horizon that reconstructs steps
over old dilemmas,
new paths over past stories.

Over the line that rests on the horizon
hope sleeps on the compass of the expected;
cradles the time the future
that at last traps our soul.

With a tempted heart
(bandaged eyes, blinded by luminosity)
I comply with the breathing that life exhales to me,
I draw strange maps,
I return to the beginning of the world.
The line that imprisons the horizon is the same one that urges
/us to walk.

Translated by Pilar Gonzalez

SEAMUS SCANLON
[IRELAND]

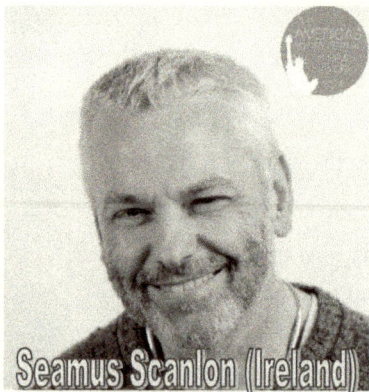

Seamus Scanlon (Ireland). Writer and librarian. He writes poetry, drama and fiction. Some of his recent achievements include a MacDowell Colony Fellowship and an Emerging Writer Fellowship from the Center for Fiction in NY. His book, *As Close As You'll Ever Be* was published in 2012. He is a tenured associate professor at The City College of New York.

Seamus Scanlon (Irlanda). Escritor y bibliotecario. Esacribe poesía, drama y ficción. Algunos de sus logros más recientes son: MacDowell Colony Fellowship y Emerging Writer Fellowship otorgada por The Center for Fiction en Nueva York. Su libro *As Close As You'll Ever Be* fue publicado en 2012. Es profesor asociado en The City College of New York.

YOU ARE THE ONE

You said it was good luck sign for us
The slick black seals breaking the surface near Nimmo's Pier.

The hard winter rain fell slow and steady.
The Corrib was in spate carrying all before it.
It was a river of sorrow that flowed through Galway,
Carrying out to sea the limp bodies of
Boys who wanted to be girls of
Girls with ripe pregnant bellies of
Shame and pain tattooed teenagers of
Women fecund with malignancies of
Men that were fighting the wide wings of black angels.
All floating out to Galway Bay and the Atlantic Ocean
All lost forever to black eels and deep channels.

I believed you about the good luck sign.

I threw my Luger far away into the river.

I said I put some boys into that water.

You said – what's done is done.

Victor you are the one.

CARLOS VELÁSQUEZ TORRES
[COLOMBIA]

Carlos Velásquez Torres (Colombia, Bogotá, 1969). Poet, translator and scholar. He earned his PhD at University of Arizona. He has published two poetry books: *Vesos del insilio* (1999) &*Es de tontos el regreso* (2004). He is currently teaching at New Mexico Highlands University.

Carlos Velásquez Torres (Colombia, Bogotá, 1969). Poeta, traductor y académico. Se doctoró en University of ArizonaHa publicado dos libros de poemas *Vesos del insilio* (1999) &*Es de tontos el regreso* (2004). En la actualidad enseña en New Mexico Highlands University.

AUC

Será la sangre más fértil
Que la hierba en el desierto
Plagado de ruinas y de tumbas
Los crucifijos
Son pasto de ganados
Enajenados por el dolor
Que escapó como alarido
De las gargantas desgarradas
Por el inmundo hierro de los esbirros
Quién será la peste
Que nos libre
Del suplicio
De la blasfemia
De la mentira a gritos
Que proclama certidumbres
Tan alocadas
Como el fragor de los traidores
En la tumba de los caídos
Aun cuando
La vergüenza
Huye aterrada por los campos
Miles de extravíos
Se regodean
Pero las puertas de emergencia
Han sido clausuradas
Para evitar una estampida
¿Habrá más obscenidad
Que presenciar impávidos el acto
Del payaso sangriento
Que nos aterró en la infancia?
El grotesco de la muerte
Cínico se posa
A nuestra diestra
Y su carcajada
Hiela la sangre del más temerario
Oh corazón
Cómo he de evitar

Que la agonía yazca ridícula
En la feria estruendosa
De mi cobardía
Y las palabras
Como ruedas locas
Siquiera perturben
La insolencia
He de abandonar mi voz
O lo que me queda de vida
Y que se disloque aún más
El estupor
Y la metralla…
El horizonte
La mirada
Y yo en medio del infierno

AUC

It must be the most fertile blood
That the weeds in the desert
Plagued by ruins and by tombs
The crucifixes
Are pastures of cattle
Left alone by the pain
That escaped like the screams
Of torn throats
By the horde's dirty steel
Who will be the pest
That will free us
From torture
From blasphemy
From the boisterous lie
That proclaims certitude
So crazed
Like the heat of the traitors
In the tomb of the fallen

Even when
The shame
Flees terrified by the camps
Thousands of losses
Pleasure themselves
But the emergency doors
Have been shut
To avoid a stampede
Is there something more obscene
Than witnessing unperturbed the act
Of the bloody clown
That horrified us in our infancy?
Death's grotesque
Poses as a cynic
At our right hand
And his laugh
Freezes the blood of the most brash
Oh heart
How should I avoid
That the agony sit ridiculously
In the thunderous fair
Of my cowardice
And my words
Like crazy wheels
Even disturb
The insolence

Translated by Pilar Gonzalez

AUGUSTO RODRÍGUEZ
[ECUADOR]

Augusto Rodríguez (Ecuador, Guayaquil, 1979). Poet and editor. He is one of the most prolific writers of his generation. Amongst his published poetry collections are: *Mientras ella mata mosquitos* (2004); *Animales salvajes* (2005); *La bestia que me habita* (2005); *Cantos contra un dinosaurio ebrio* (2007); *Voy hacia mi cuerpo* (2010); *Las islas vírgenes de tu cuerpo* (2011); *La enfermedad invisible* (2012); *Las águilas del adiós* (2012); *Mi patria es la irrealidad* (2012); *El libro del cáncer* (2012) &*El libro de la enfermedad* (2013).

Augusto Rodríguez (Ecuador, Guayaquil, 1979). Poeta y editor. Es uno de los escritores más prolíficos de su generación. Entre sus libros de poemas publicados están: *Mientras ella mata mosquitos* (2004); *Animales salvajes* (2005); *La bestia que me habita* (2005); *Cantos contra un dinosaurio ebrio* (2007); *Voy hacia mi cuerpo* (2010); *Las islas vírgenes de tu cuerpo* (2011); *La enfermedad invisible* (2012); *Las águilas del adiós* (2012); *Mi patria es la irrealidad* (2012); *El libro del cáncer* (2012) &*El libro de la enfermedad* (2013).

WHEN I COME HOME

When I come home
I see ramshackle houses
cats on the corners
garbage in the streets
men hanging from their own ties
dogs flying like birds
trees philosophizing with ghosts
the dead thinking they are archangels
flies breeding cockroaches
men surviving.

When I come home
nostalgia cannot sleep
memories flow through my mind
and the embrace of my father, dead,
who eagerly asks:
How are you, son of all my hopes?

ROSANA ACQUARONI
[ESPAÑA]

Rosana Acquaroni (España, Madrid, 1964). Poet, visual artist and educator. She earned a doctorate in applied linguistics at Universidad Complutense de Madrid. She has published five poetry collections: *Del mar bajo los puentes* (1988); *El jardín navegable* (1990); *Cartografía sin mundo* (1995); *Lámparas de arena* (2000); *Discordia de los dóciles* (2011). Her poems have been translated to several languages and received literary awards.

Rosana Acquaroni (España, Madrid, 1964). Poeta, artista visual y educadora. Recibió un doctorado en lingüística aplicada en la Universidad Complutense de Madrid. Ha publicado cuatro libros de poemas: *Del mar bajo los puentes* (1988); *El jardín navegable* (1990); *Cartografía sin mundo* (1995); *Lámparas de arena* (2000); *Discordia de los dóciles* (2011). Sus poemas han recibido premios literarios y han sido traducidos a varias lenguas.

Po-ética

Hay un tiempo
en que la leña arde en el paraíso
climatizado
de los seres prudentes.
En un mundo sensato
comedido
donde ya nada nuevo es necesario.

Un momento preciso
para volver a casa cada día
y rebañar a solas
la miel del desencanto,
la rebanada fría del dolor.

Dentro de tu edificio
hay una vibración imperceptible
que avanza sin querer,
como un desprendimiento
de nieve encadenada
que quisiera cegar la oscuridad.

Es el frágil temblor
de un alud que iniciara
su descenso,
la quemadura blanca
de una noche interior que se vacía
en el mismo momento en que la nieve
desbroza su letargo,
su breve oscuridad,
y una niña olvidada
sostiene en algún mundo una cerilla,
minúscula claridad
que emana de la sombra y del silencio.

La clarividencia de la noche
borra los espejismos de la luz.

Ya sólo es cierto
que esa luz nos obliga
a descalzar el alma,
a contemplar por fin
la otra claridad,
aquella que se esconde tras la luz.

(Discordia de los dóciles, 2011)

RALPH NAZARETH
[INDIA]

Ralph Nazareth (India, Mangalore). Poet, editor and scholar. He is a professor of English at Nassau Community College. He is also the managing editor of Yuganta Press in Stamford. For the past six years, he's been a volunteer teacher of creative writing at Green Haven, a maximum security prison in upstate New York. His poetry collection *Ferrying Secrets* was published in India in 2005.

Ralph Nazareth (India, Mangalore). Poeta, editor y académico. Es profesor de inglés en Nassau Community College. También es el editor en jefe de Yuganta Press en Stamford. Desde hace seis años ha sido profesor voluntario de escritura creativa en la cárcel de máxima seguridad en Green Haven del estado de Nueva York. Su libro de poemas *Ferrying Secrets* fue publicado en India en 2005.

How come the earth spins

My daughter says the whole world's attached:
the steps she's sitting on to the sidewalk,
the sidewalk to the street,
the street to Joey's block,
and Joey's block to the railroad track
which goes on forever,
attaching everything every which way.
Round and round the world it goes,
wrapping its silver ribbons.
That's how come the earth spins,
attaching sea to land
and land to sky.
The sun, she knows, is attached to the earth;
the stars too, which are also attached to heaven,
where God lives, attached to his bolts of lightning,
which she hates,
and his rainbow lollipops,
which she loves.
My daughter's America is attached to my India
by an invisible thread, she thinks,
and India to the elephants and tigers
and also to its poor people
and beyond that she does not know
except the whole world's for sure attached.

She's been told she was once attached to her mother.
She'd like to know why she wasn't attached to me.
I say I had to let go.
"Are you attached to anything?" she asks.
"How about to my seat?" I answer.
"Pa," she scolds me, "not like that,
but, you know, like when you sleep
so close to Ma at night
or to me when I have horrible dreams."

The whole world's attached
'cus if it wasn't, it would come apart

and go to pieces.
How does she know?
But she does.
Though she doesn't yet know
about life with a capital L,
she knows that "attached"
has something to do with a gift.
Karen's mom told her,
but for the life of her,
she cannot remember its name.

¿CÓMO ES POSIBLE QUE LA TIERRA DE VUELTAS?

Mi hija dice que el mundo entero está atado:
El peldaño donde está sentada está atado a la acera,
La acera está atada a la calle,
La calle al bloque de Joey,
Y el bloque de Joey a los rieles del tren,
Lo cual sigue y sigue infinitamente,
atando todo a todo de esta manera.

Redondo y redondo el mundo sigue,
enrostrando su cinta plateada.
Así es como el planeta da vueltas,
atando el mar y la tierra
Y la tierra al cielo.
Ella sabe que el sol está atado al planeta;
Y las estrellas también, las cuales a su vez
están atadas al paraíso,
donde vive Dios, atado a sus ráfagas de relámpagos,
que ella odia,
y a los arcoíris,
que ella ama.
La América de mi hija está atada a mi India
por una cinta invisible, piensa ella,
y la india está atada a los elefantes y los tigres

y también a su gente pobre
y más allá de eso ella no sabe
excepto que el mundo entero está atado.

Alguien le ha dicho que una vez ella estuvo atada a su madre.
Ella quiere saber por qué no estuvo atada a mí también.
Le digo que tengo que dejar ir.
"¿Estás atado a alguna cosa?
"¿A mi silla quizás?" Le contesto.
"Pa," me regaña," no así
tú ya sabes, como cuando duermes
tan cerca de Ma por las noches
o cerca de mi cuando tengo sueños horribles."

El mundo entero está atado
porque si no, se desgranaría
partiéndose en mil pedazos.
¿Cómo sabe ella?
Lo sabe y eso es todo.
Aunque todavía no conoce
nada de la vida con L mayúscula,
Ella sabe que "atado"
tiene algo que ver con regalo.
La mama de Karen se lo dijo,
Aunque ella, por nada del mundo,
puede recordar su nombre.

MERCEDES ROFFÉ
[ARGENTINA]

Mercedes Roffé (Argentina, 1954)
Poet, translator and editor. She has
received numerous distinctions
such as the Guggenheim (2001)
and the Civitella Ranieri (2012)
fellowships. Some of her most no-
torious poetry books are: *El tapiz*
(1983); *Cámara baja* (1987); *La
noche y las palabras* (1996); *Can-
to errante* (2002); *Memorial de
agravios* (2002), *La ópera fantasma*
(2005) and *Las linternas flotantes*
(2009). Several of her poetry collections have been translated and published
in Quebec, England, Italy and Romania. She is also the director of Ediciones
Pen Press.

Mercedes Roffé (Argentina, 1954) Poeta, traductora y editora. Ha recibi-
do numerosas distinciones como las becas Guggenheim (2001) y Civite-
lla Ranieri (2012). Algunos de sus libros de poemas más notorios son *El
tapiz* (1983); *Cámara baja* (1987); *La noche y las palabras* (1996); *Canto
errante* (2002); *Memorial de agravios* (2002), *La ópera fantasma* (2005) y
Las linternas flotantes (2009). Varios de sus libros han sido traducidos y
publicados en Quebec, Inglaterra, Italia y Rumania. También es directora
de Ediciones Pen Press.

Lotus

Enlightened
are called
those who
their lids [sewn]
their lips
half open
count / see
the petals
opening / falling
of a deceitful
s u m p t u o u s
flower
in the uncertain ground
that
what is to come
reserves
for memory

(Translated by Judith Filc)

Loto

Iluminados
se llama
a aquellos que
los párpados [cosidos]
entreabiertos
los labios
cuentan / ven
abrirse / caer
los pétalos
de una mentida flor
s u n t u o s a
en el incierto paraje
que
lo por venir
le guarda
a la memoria

DANIEL SHAPIRO
[USA]

Daniel Shapiro is the author of the poetry collections *Child with a Swan's Wings* (2013), *The Red Handkerchief and Other Poems* (2014), and "Woman at the Cusp of Twilight" (unpublished). His translation of Chilean poet Tomás Harris's *Cipango* (2010) received a starred review in *Library Journal*. His poetry, prose, and translations have been published in journals including *American Book Review*, *American Poetry Review*, *Black Warrior Review*, *BOMB*, and *The Brooklyn Rail*, and in the anthologies *Mexico: A Traveler's Literary Companion*, *Vapor Transatlántico/Tramp Steamer*, and *The Oxford Book of Latin American Poetry*. He has received fellowships from the National Endowment for the Arts and PEN to translate *Cipango* and Roberto Ransom's *Desaparecidos, animales y artistas* (Missing Persons, Animals and Artists). Shapiro serves as Director of Literature and Editor of *Review: Literature and Arts of the Americas* at the Americas Society in New York.

Daniel Shapiro es autor de los libros de poemas *Child with a Swan's Wings* (2013), *The Red Handkerchief and Other Poems* (2014) y "Woman at the Cusp of Twilight" (inédito). Su traducción de *Cipango* (2010) del poeta chileno Tomás Harris recibió excelente crítica en *Library Journal*. Su poesía y su prosa han sido publicadas en *American Book Review*, *American Poetry Review*, *Black Warrior Review*, *BOMB*, y *The Brooklyn Rail*. También se ha incluido su trabajo en las antologías *Mexico: A Traveler's Literary Companion*, *Vapor Transatlántico/Tramp Steamer* y *The Oxford Book of Latin American Poetry*. Ha recibido becas de National Endowment for the Arts y PEN para traducir *Cipango* y el libro *Desaparecidos, animales y artistas* de Roberto Ransom. Shapiro se desempeña como director de Literatura y editor de *Review: Literature and Arts of the Americas* en the Americas Society, New York.

NUMBERS AND ROOMS

I began as something shameful, something flawed,
when I faced the stark reflection of myself
in the gold bathroom mirror, kept my mouth closed
in fear, saw my father's jaw drop open
when he'd spring my door, inside a lover
piled on me, the window screened by oleander.

I rode asphalt crests through hills that summer,
stink of skunk-spray, aloe, honeysuckle, cows.
I parked—lights flicked through smog—eased down my zipper.

I rode all night in a white Camaro
with a young Filipino who picked me up
in the Brass Rail. He pushed my head to his lap

and made me love it, made me see my body
furtively, growing, shrinking from itself.
When he rolled the white door open, I rolled free.

Seeking what? Sidling into nights unseen,
cruising men with molded torsos guiding their hips
through huge underground discos, one-night scenes,

a fraud to myself. Where else if not here
could eyes dart black pools of mirrors, numbers and rooms
where another pair of eyes waited for me?

The stiff plunge in beneath a whirring fan.
Afterwards, the twin robes printed with cranes.
Too scared of what I was, what I might be,

the naked fear of discovery,
(which, in my flight home, pitted me against sunrise
and the dignity of tenderness)

to feel what a man might feel for a man
in the flash of seed sprung from willing triggers
dueled beneath our faces dumb with pleasure.

JOANNA C. VALENTE
[USA]

Joanna C. Valente lives in Brooklyn, New York. She is the author of *Sirs & Madams*, forthcoming from Aldrich Press in late 2014. She is also the Founding & Chief Editor of *Yes Poetry*, as well as a columnist for *Luna Luna Magazine*. In her spare time, she is a mermaid.

Joanna C. Valente vive en Brooklyn, Nueva York. Es la autora de *Sirs & Madams* que se publicará por Aldrich Press a finales de 2014. Además, es la fundadora y editora en jefe de *Yes Poetry* y columnista de *Luna Luna Magazine*. En su tiempo libre es una sirena.

NO ONE LIKES YOU UNTIL YOU'RE DEAD

in Coney Island, there is a body
stranded on uneven sand making love
to earth, polluted space.

A woman's hands smell like plastic
suntan lotion bottles. Swarms of
moths stroke her back, wings

whirring like a smile. Why bother
blocking rays when the cancer's
already there?

She swats them with her plastic
Chinese fan from the corner 99 cent
store, thinking about the hands

who make dollar store dreams.

LUIS ALBERTO AMBROGGIO
[ARGENTINA-USA]

Luis Alberto Ambroggio is an internationally known Hispanic-American poet classified by Casa the America as "a prominent representative of the avant-garde of Hispanic-American poetry in the U.S.". He is the author of seventeen collections of poetry published in the United States and abroad. Ambroggio was appointed as a member of the North American Academy of the Spanish Language, the Royal Spanish Academy (RAE) and PEN. His latest books of poetry among others, *Difficult Beauty: Selected Poems 1987-2006 (2009)*, with an introduction by Pulitzer Prize winner Oscar Hijuelos and *The Wind's Archeology* (2011: winner of the 2013 International Latino Best Book Award), *We are all Whitman,* have been widely praised in Europe, the US (*Diario de las Americas*) and Latin America. Others awards include the 2004 Spanish TV Award for poems on solitude, Fulbright-Hayes, Simón Bolivar. His poetry and essays have appeared in newspapers, magazines (including *Passport, Scholastic, International Poetry Review,* and *Hispanic Culture Review*), poetry anthologies, textbooks (*Paisajes, Bridges to Literature, Voices: Breaking Down Barriers)* and award-winning electronic collections of Latino Literature *(Alexander Street Press).* His poetry, translated into several languages, is the subject of several books and courses and has been selected for the Archives of Hispanic-American Literature of the Library of Congress.

Luis Alberto Ambroggio es un escritor, poeta, ensayista, clasificado por la Casa de América como "Representante destacado en la vanguardia de la poesía hispanoamericana en los Estados Unidos". Miembro de la RAE, del PEN y Presidente de la Delegación en Washington D.C. de la Academia Norteamericana de la Lengua Española. Cuenta con reconocimientos y premios de la TVE, Simón Bolívar, Fullbright-Hays, de la Hispanic National Honor Society, del Instituto y Patrimonio Cultural Rubén Darío, entre otros y más de veinte libros publicados, incluyendo *Todos somos Whitman,* las versiones bilingües *Difficult Beauty: Selected poems* 1987-2006, prólogo del premio Pulitzer Oscar Hijuelos (2009) y *La arqueología del Viento* (2011: ganadora del 2013 International Latino Best book Award), Sus ensayos y poemas han aparecido en periódicos, revistas (como *Passport, Scholastic, International Poetry Review, Hispanic Culture Review*), antologías y manuales (*Cool Salsa,Paisajes, Bridges to Literature,Voices*) y colecciones electrónicas premiadas *de* Literatura *(Alexander Street Press).* Su obra poética, congregada en el volumen *En el Jardín de los vientos. Obra poética (1974-2014)* publicado por la Academia de la Lengua, ha sido objeto de cursos, libros de crítica literaria, traducida a más de 10 idiomas y seleccionada para el Archivo de Literatura Hispanoamericana de la Biblioteca del Congreso.

THEIR DOVE-SONG HURTS

he, whose infinite girth is encircled by midnight, noon
-Juan Ramón Jimenez

Pilot of failures and ambitions
I have come to cleave
the pure night.
The moon enticed by dusk
illuminates joy
with a full, pale face
like one in love.

Beneath the moon and sun
desires navigate in gondolas.
Love's ghosts
do acrobatics without contours
nightingales or mornings.

Later you can hear the weightless dew
of unsleeping souls.

In the atmosphere we are kept awake by masks
that exhume cries.

Their dove-song hurts
when dusk sinks
to the bottom of the long night.

We all fly to decipher bit by bit
that perplexing color
in which we are a shadow
and a turbulent feather.

©Luis Alberto Ambroggio (from Difficult Beauty, 2009)
(Translated by Yvette Neisser Moreno)

SU CANTO DE PALOMA DUELE

> *"él, a cuyo infinito alrededor se ciñen*
> *la medianoche, el mediodía"*
> -Juan Ramón Jimenez

Piloto de fracasos y ambiciones
he venido a surcar
la noche pura.
La luna engolosinada
con el crepúsculo
luce como enamorada el regocijo
con cara llena y pálida.

Bajo la luna y el sol
navegan los deseos en góndolas.
Los fantasmas del amor
hacen acrobacias sin contornos
ruiseñores y mañanas.

Luego se escucha el rocío levísimo
de almas que no duermen.

En el medio nos desvelan las máscaras
que exhuman gritos.

Su canto de paloma duele
cuando se hunde el crepúsculo
hasta el fondo de la noche larga.

Todos volamos para descifrar poco a poco
ese color perplejo
del que somos una sombra
y una pluma turbulenta.

©Luis Alberto Ambroggio (de El Testigo se desnuda 2002).

MARTA LÓPEZ-LUACES
[ESPAÑA]

Marta López-Luaces was born in A Coruña, Spain, in 1964. She is a novelist, poet, and translator. She holds a Ph. D. in Spanish and Latin American Literature from NYU (2000). She has published three books of poetry: *Distancias y destierros* (1998), *Las lenguas del viajero* (2005) and *Los arquitectos de lo imaginario* (2011)and a *plaquette* entitled *Memorias de un vacío* (2000). *Los arquitectos de lo imaginario* was finalist of the prestigious award Ausiás March (2011). A selection of her work was translated into Romanian and published under the title *Pravalirea foculi* (2010). Her poetry was also translated into Italian under the title of *Accento Magico* (2002). The translator Gary Recz just finished translating *Los arquitectos de lo imaginario* into English. She has translated from English into Spanish *Selected Works* from Robert Duncan (Madrid: Bartleby, 2011). She is the co-director of *Galerna*, a Spanish-language literary journal. She published the collection of short stories, *La Virgen de la Noche* and Vaso Roto just published her novel *Los traductores del viento* in November.

Marta López-Luaces (A Coruña, España 1964) obtuvo su Ph D en 2000 por New York University. Ha publicado los siguientes libros libros de poesía: *Distancia y destierros* (1998), *Las lenguas del viajero* (2005), *Los arquitectos de lo imaginario* (2011) y la plaqueta *Memorias de un vacío* (2000). *Los arquitectos de lo imaginario* fue finalist del prestigioso premio Ausiás March (2011). Una selección de su obra fue traducida al rumano y publicada bajo el título *Pravalirea foculi* (2010). Su poesía también se tradujo al italiano con el título *Accento Magico* (2002). Gary Recz acaba de terminar la traducción al inglés de *Los arquitectos de lo imaginario.* Marta López-Luaces ha traducido del inglés al español *Selected Works* de Robert Duncan (2011). Es codirectora de la revista literaria *Galerna*. Ha publicado la colección de historias *La Virgen de la Noche*. La editorial Vaso Roto acaba de publicar, en noviembre, su novela *Los traductores del viento*.

TEMPESTADES

Who let the light into the dark?
Began the many movements of the passion?
Robert Duncan

Venía de nosotros,
del viento y su ulular.

En la cresta de la brisa
la tormenta
asedió
la firma de las cosas
convocó el temor a lo Bello
traición de lo diáfano.

Venía de nosotros
y violó el orden
de la Eternidad.

En la cresta
de la Tormenta
el gris.

STORMS

> *Who let the light into the dark?*
> *Began the many movements of the passion?*
>
> Robert Duncan

It arose within us,
from the wind and its ululation.

On the crest of the breeze
the storm
laid siege
to matter's own signature,
summoning a terror of Beauty
and betrayal of all things diaphanous.

It arose within us,
violating the order
of Eternity.

On the crest
of the Storm
rests the gray.

MARIANELA MEDRANO
[R. DOMINICANA]

Marianela Medrano is a Dominican writer and poet, with a PhD in psychology living in Connecticut since 1990. Her individual publications include: *Oficio de Vivir* (Buho,1986), *Los Alegres Ojos de la Tristeza* (1987), *Regando Esencias/ The Scent of Waiting* (1998), *Curada de Espantos* (2002), *Diosas de la Yuca*, (2011), and *Prietica* (2013). Medrano's work also appears in literary magazines and academic journals such as *Brooklyn Review* (1995), *Punto 7 Review* (1996) *Sisters of Caliban* (1996) *Callaloo* (2000), *Tertuliando/Hanging Out*(1997), *Letras Femeninas* (2005), *Kacike* (2009) *Trivia Voices of Feminism* (2009), *Journal of Poetry Therapy* (2010), *Sandplay Therapy Journal* (2010), *The Afro-Latin@ Reader* (2010), *Letralia* (2011), *Phatitude* (2012), *Mujeres Como Islas II* (2012), among others.

Marianela Medrano es dominicana y vive en Connecticut (Estados Unidos) desde 1990. Es doctora en Psicología. Frecuentemente ofrece talleres de poesía/literatura y temas de salud mental en diferentes universidades y centros culturales en los Estados Unidos. Tiene publicados los siguientes libros: *Oficio de Vivir* (1986), *Los Alegres Ojos de la Tristeza* (1987), *Regando Esencias/ The Scent of Waiting* (1998) y *Curada de Espantos* (2002), *Diosas de la Yuca* (2011) y *Prietica* (2013). Su trabajo ha sido publicado en diferentes antologías y revistas incluyendo: *Brooklyn Review* (1995), *Punto 7 Review* (1996) *Sisters of Caliban* (1996) *Callaloo* (2000), *Tertuliando/Hanging Out*(1997), *Letras Femeninas* (2005), *Kacike* (2009) *Trivia Voices of Feminism* (2009), *Journal of Poetry Therapy* (2010), *Sandplay Therapy Journal* (2010), *The Afro-Latin@ Reader* (2010), *Letralia* (2011), *Phatitude* (2012), *Mujeres Como Islas II* (2012) entre otros.

Of how we learned to play hide and seek

*I so they would trust us, because I knew they were people who would convert
to our faith, with love and not by force, gave them some red berets and some
glass stones and many other worthless things.*
Christopher Columbus -*Diary of Navigation* –

In the lie of red berets
the silky black pretends its disappearance
later on it comes out for air in the miracle of the
kinky texture of the African consolation
Ochùn inhales us with divine force

In the fragmentation of glass we seem to succumb
until we discover the magic of stained glass
filtering the hot rays of the Grand Sun
In the spacious vortex of cathedrals we fly
pray the Holy Father in order to sing to *Yocahù*
In the background of the Holy Mary
vibrates*Atabey's* ethereal and fluid figure

The island herself from time to time
seems to coil up in the sadness
her body a bloody river moist the Grand Sun
-that is why our dusks are so beautiful-

In the roots of the yucca
the goddesses and the gods keep on making miracles
Caguama protects us in her untamable conch
even in these days of beaches colonized by tourists
Playful and calm people
We play under the colorless skins of the saints
to protect our golden epidermis.

Translated by the author and Janet E. Aalfs
From *Diosas de la Yuca*, (Torremozas, 2011)

DE CÓMO APRENDIMOS EL JUEGO AL ESCONDITE

Yo porque nos tuviesen mucha amistad, porque conocí que era gente que
se convertiría a nuestra Santa Fé con amor que no por fuerza les di a algunos
de ellos unos bonetes colorados y unas cuentas de vidrio y otras cosas muchas
de poco valor.
Cristóbal Colón -*Diario de Navegación –*

En la mentira de bonetes colorados
simula esconderse el sedoso azabache
más tarde sale a tomar aire en el milagro de la
textura hirsuta del consuelo africano
Ochùn nos inhala con fuerza divina

En la fragmentación del vidrio parecemos abatirnos
hasta descubrir el milagroso colorido de los vitrales
filtrando los rayos calientes del Gran Sol
En el espacioso vórtice de las catedrales volamos
rezamos el padrenuestro para cantarle a Yocahù
Detrás del avemaría vibra la figura
incorpórea fluida de Atabey

La isla misma de vez en cuando
parece enroscarse en la tristeza
su cuerpo de río ensangrentado empapa al Gran Sol
-por eso son tan hermosos nuestros atardeceres-

En las raíces de la yuca
las diosas y los dioses continúan haciendo milagros
Caguama nos resguarda en su carapacho indomable
aún en estos días de playas colonizadas por turistas
Gente retozona y calmada
jugamos bajo las pieles descoloridas de los santos
para proteger nuestra epidermis dorada.

ELY ROSA ZAMORA
[VENEZUELA]

Ely Rosa Zamora was born in Venezuela and has lived in New York since 1998. She is a graduate of Escuela Nacional de Artes Escénicas de Caracas and holds an MFA in Creative Writing in Spanish from New York University. She is the author of the poetry collections *Paz Obscena* (2008,) *Semilla* (2009,) *Detrito Olvidado/Forgotten Detritus;* a book of poetry and photographs in collaboration with artist Barbara Madsen (2009,) *No Tongue/Sin lengua* (2011,) and *Sin lengua y otras imposibilidades dramáticas* (2013). Her work has been presented in Argentina, England, Italy, and the United States. Her poetry is included in the Anthology *"Voces para Lilith"* Literatura contemporánea de temática lésbica en Sudamérica, (2011.) She currently teaches in the Spanish Department at Rutgers University.

Ely Rosa Zamora nació en Venezuela y vive en Nueva York desde 1998. Es egresada de la Escuela Nacional de Artes Escénicas de Caracas y tiene una maestría en escritura creativa de New York University. Ha escrito dos plaquetas *Paz obscena* (2008), *Semilla (2009)*. Ha publicado también *Detrito olvidado/Forgotten Detritus*, un libro de poesía y fotografía en colaboración con la artista Barbara Madsen (2009), *Sin lengua/ No Tongue* (2011) y *Sin lengua y otras imposibilidades dramáticas* (2013). Su trabajo se ha presentado en Argentina, Inglaterra, Italia y USA. Su poesía fue incluida en la antología *"Voces para Lilith" Literatura contemporánea de temática lésbica en Sudamérica* (2011). En la actualidad enseña en el Departamento de Español de Rutgers University.

Helmi contemplates photos of the body of his son, there is nothing else.
The Cyclops is sinking into his own eye.
When he came home, he did not recognize it, the soldiers have shit everywhere.
In the darkness there is no fear sniffing the lilies bitten by dogs, the smell also finds its hideout.
With a hole in his knee, Helmi runs looking for his home, until he bleeds to death.
This pain, is not pain on the other, it is my own pain.

(Translated by the author)

Helmi contempla las fotos del cadáver de su hijo; no hay otras
El cíclope va hundiéndose en su propio ojo
Cuando entró a su casa no la reconoció; los soldados se habían cagado por todas partes
En la oscuridad no se teme olfatear los lirios mordidos por los perros; el olor también encuentra su escondite
Con un hueco en la rodilla, Helmi corre buscando su casa y muere desangrado
Este dolor no es un dolor por el otro; es mi propio dolor.

SUSANA ADA VILLALBA
[ARGENTINA]

Susana Ada Villalba is an Argentinean poet, playwright and cultural activist. She has published six poetry collections; among them are *Susy, secretos del corazón,Matar un animal,* and *Plegarias.* She is the director of Casa de la Lectura of Buenos Aires. In 2011, she received the Guggenheim Fellowship. Susana teaches graduate courses on poetry and theater. Also, she curates and presents the web based poetry radio show of the National Library of Argentina. She founded and directed the Casa de la Poesía in Buenos Aires, the Casa Nacional de la Poesía in Argentina and their poetry festivals.

Susana Ada Villalba es una poeta, dramaturga y gestora cultural argentina. Ha publicado sir libros de poemas entre lo que se incluyen: *Susy, secretos del corazón,Matar un animal* y *Plegarias.* Es la directora de Casa de la Lectura del Gobierno de la Ciudad de Buenos Aires. En 2011 recibió la beca Guggenheim. Susana enseña cursos graduados sobre poesía y teatro. También cura y presenta un programa radial de poesía página WEB de la Biblioteca Nacional. Fundó y dirigió la Casa de la Poesía de la Ciudad de Buenos Aires y la Casa Nacional de la Poesía en Argentina y sus Festivales Internacionales.

THE STONE (FRAGMENT)

holding in silence
as love
is an art

would the sea be the sea
if I did not keep it back?

something intangible
as water
defeats me
its transparency
would the sea exist
if it did not confront me?

dreaming
without getting lost
is an art
sometimes a rock
shudders
before the lost cliff
even the irreducible
can be amalgamated
that is love
a topaz vein
surprises you
in the porphyry
what did you think
gold was
but a scar?

the rupture
is infinite

edges
are vagues

everything is a fragment of

dust from the stones sense
if my love is forever
also my solitude

incorruptible
gravitating in the space
of differentiation

based on myself
I am not still
everything attracts me
equally

the sky is a pampa

the star magnet
is its distance
I am intrinsic

the art of being
still
is to surrender the heart
to movement
the wind whistles
an echo
of what my detachment
has announced before

would the water sing
if it did not go through me?

Translated by Patricia Scolieri and Susana Villalba

LA PIEDRA (FRAGMENTO)

sostener en silencio
como amar
es un arte

¿existiría el mar
si no lo contuviera?

me derrota
algo intangible
como el agua

su transparencia
¿si no me enfrentara
existiría el mar?

soñar sin perderse
es un arte
a veces una roca
se estremece contra la orilla
perdida
hasta lo irreductible
se amalgama

amar es eso
y te sorprende
un filón de topacio
en el porfirio
entonces qué creías
que es el oro
sino la cicatriz

es infinita
la ruptura

los bordes
son difusos

todo es fragmento
polvo del sentido
de las piedras
si mi amor es eterno
también la soledad
incorruptible
gravitando en el espacio
de la separación

sostenida de mí

no estoy quieta
todo me atrae por igual

el cielo es una pampa

el imán de la estrella
es su distancia
soy intrínseca

el arte de estar
quieta
es dar el corazón
al movimiento
silba el viento
un eco
de lo que ya anunciaba
mi desprendimiento

¿cantaría el agua
si no me atravesara?

CARLOS MANUEL RIVERA
[PUERTO RICO]

Carlos Manuel Rivera (Carboinael Rixema) was born in Puerto Rico. He is a poet, actor, performer and college professor. In 2000, he received a PhD. in Latin American and Caribbean Literature from Arizona State University. In 2013, he was awarded the Premio Internacional de Literatura by the Instituto de Cultura Puertorriqueña in essay. His poetry has been published in literary magazines such as: *Campo de los Patos, Sable, Claridad En Rojo, Oasis, Abya Yala* and *Taller Literario, as well as the anthologies San Diego Poetry, The Best of Panic. ¡En vivo from the East Village!, 8va Convergencia Internacional de Poemas Juninpais, Homenaje a la profesora L. Teresa Valdivieso* and *500 Otounos de Prosa y Verso*. He has published the books *Teatro popular: El Nuevo Teatro Pobre de América de Pedro Santaliz* (2005) and the performance poetry collection *Soplo mágicos disparates* (2003). In 2010, he recorded his poems and performances in a CD entitled *ASI MI NATION*. He is currently an associate professor of Spanish at Bronx Community College, CUNY.

Carlos Manuel Rivera (Carboinael Rixema) nació en Puerto Rico. Es poeta, actor y performero, como también profesor universitario e investigador. Obtuvo su grado doctoral en literatura latinoamericana y del Caribe hispano de la Universidad Estatal de Arizona (2000). Obtuvo el Premio Internacional de Literatura 2013 del Instituto de Cultura Puertorriqueña en la categoría de ensayo. Ha publicado su poesía en las revistas literarias: *Campo de los Patos, Sable, Claridad En Rojo, Oasis, Abya Yala* y *Taller Literario, como* en las antologías, *San Diego Poetry, The Best of Panic. ¡En vivo from the East*

Village!,8va Convergencia Internacional de Poemas Juninpais, Homenaje a la profesora L. Teresa Valdivieso y *500 Otounos de Prosa y Verso*. Tiene publicado su libro de investigación *Teatro popular: El Nuevo Teatro Pobre de América de Pedro Santaliz* (2005) y el de poemas-performances, *Soplo mágicos disparates* (2003). Además grabó su CD de poemas y performances *ASI MI NATION* (2010). Actualmente es Catedrático Asociado de Español en Bronx Community College, CUNY.

OF GOODNESS AND ADVENTURES

To a friend: Consuelo Astete

Happy are those who
facing a morning
hear in the trill
their sins.

Happy are those who
in the air
smooth with their hands
the useful embroidery of their fright.

Happy are those who
through their shadows
recognize of the firm stem
the value of the nest in the chrysalis.

Happy are those who
extract from roses
their dynamic solace
and beautify their palms.

Happy are those who
in a somnific stroll
go to their house
and determine their dwelling.

Happy are those who
stir their alembic
and see of the moon
the magnitude of its illusion.

Happy are all
of us who scent
paths and scale hills
without falling into homage.

DE BIEN Y AVENTURAS

A una amiga: Consuelo Astete

Felices, los que
ante una mañana
oyen de trinos
sus pecados.

Felices, los que
en el aire
suavizan con sus manos
el labrado útil de su espanto.

Felices, los que
a través de sus sombras
reconocen del tallo
el valor de nido en la crisálida.

Felices, los que
manejan de rosas
su quietud dinámica
y embellecen sus palmeras.

Felices, los que
en andar soñoliento

van a su casa
y determinan su morada.

Felices, los que
menean su alambique
y ven de luna
su magnitud de quimera.

Felices, todos
los que olfateamos
veredas y adelantamos colinas
sin descender de homenajes.

FRANCISCO X. FERNÁNDEZ NAVAL
[ESPAÑA]

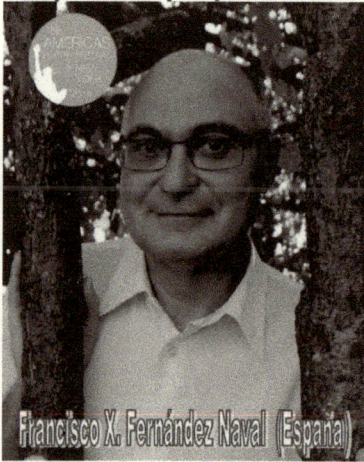

Francisco X. Fernández Naval (Ourense- Spain, 1956), poet and storyteller. He is the author of a vast production in the Galician language that includes: poetry, novels, stories, essays, children literature, youth fiction, travel guides, theater and film scripts. Some of his works have been translated to other languages such as Castilian, French, English, Euskara, Catalan, Arabic and Portuguese.

Francisco X. Fernández Naval (Ourense- España, 1956), poeta y narrador. Autor de una amplia obra en lengua gallega, que incluye poesía, novela, libros de relatos, ensayo, literatura infantil, juvenil y de viajes, guiones cinematográficos y teatro. Algunos títulos fueron traducidos a otras lenguas, entre ellas, castellano, francés, inglés, vasco, catalán, árabe y portugués.

SEA OF LIRA

Wide, the sea of Lira,
filling all there is from eye to eye,
from Foz and Forcados to the river that dies in the mouth
like a hooked fish.
A sea with an attitude, this sea;
it has its days, like one has.
The sea of Lira
is low and deep
when seen from afar,
keeps a glimpse of sails in Anguieira
and a nostalgia of hugs
in the stony guts of seagulls.
Is quaking bog, field to sail, threshing yard for sloops,
beach of spread whales, path and plain
to go outside the island
—to that spot, where Ricardo died.

In the sea of Lira there are drowned sorrows,
dried grieves, memories that forgot
the sequence of the waves, and now sleep
in the blue shade of Cabaleiras;
A place of stern rocks, seed of bulbous seaweed,
caulkers' teeth. The sea of Lira
has a scent of old salting, a time to name,
a scent of hope and waiting.

MAR DE LIRA

O mar de Lira é ancho,
ocupa a vista toda que se abrangue entre os ollos,
dende Foz e os Forcados ata o río que morre de
boca

coma un peixe encarnado.
Mar de carácter
ten días, coma un home.
O mar de Lira é baixo e fondo
se se mira de lonxe,
garda un brillo de velas na Anguieira
e unha nostalxia de abrazos
no calcáreo pandullo das gavotas.
É lameiro, leira de navegar, eira de barcas,
ribeira de baleas derramadas, carreiro e chaira
para fóra da illa
-o lugar no que morreu Ricardo-

No mar de Lira hai penas afogadas
mágoas secas, memorias que esqueceron
a sucesión das ondas e hoxe dormen
na sombra azul das Cabaleiras.
Lugar de petóns feros, semente de verdello,
dentes de galafato, o mar de Lira
recende a salga vella, tempo de nomear,
a esperanza e as esperas.

DAVID GROFF
[USA]

David Groff's book of poems *Clay* was chosen by Michael Waters as winner of the Louise Bogan Award and published in 2013 by Trio House Press. His previous collection, *Theory of Devolution*, published in 2002 by the University of Illinois Press, was selected by Mark Doty for the National Poetry Series. Both books were finalists for the Lambda Literary Award. He has co-edited two anthologies, the Lambda-winning *Who's Yer Daddy?: Gay Writers Celebrate Their Mentors and Forerunners* (University of Wisconsin Press) and *Persistent Voices: Poetry by Writers Lost to AIDS* (Alyson). For his friend Robin Hardy, he completed the book *The Crisis of Desire: AIDS and the Fate of Gay Brotherhood*, which was published by Houghton Mifflin and the University of Minnesota Press. David received his MFA from the Iowa Writers Workshop and his MA in English from the University of Iowa. He is an independent editor, book and publishing consultant and teaches in the M.F.A. creative writing program of the City College of New York.

El libro *Clay* de David Groff fue seleccionado por Michael Waters como el ganador del premio Louise Bogan y publicado en 2013 por Trio House Press. Su colección anterior, *Theory of Devolution* publicada en 2002 por University of Illinois Press, fue escogida por Mark Doty para hacer parte de [The] National Poetry Series. Ambos libros fueron finalistas en el premio Lambda. David ha coeditado dos antologías, la ganadora del premio Lambda *Who's Yer Daddy?: Gay Writers Celebrate Their Mentors and Forerunners* (University of Wisconsin Press) and *Persistent Voices: Poetry by Writers Lost to AIDS* (Alyson). En nombre de su amigo Robin Hardy, terminó el libro *The*

Crisis of Desire: AIDS and the Fate of Gay Brotherhood que fue publicado por Houghton Mifflin y University of Minnesota Press. Recibió un MFA del Iowa Writers Workshop y un MA en Inglés de la Universidad de Iowa. Es editor independiente, consultor de publicaciones y enseña en el programa de maestría en escritura creativa (MFA) en The City College of New York.

CLAY'S FACE IS

a thinned blade
used hard,

scalpel and scalpel's
consequence,

boxers in the clinch,
squeezing out inessence

until blade or virus gasps,
respires.

His labial skin
swags him: the pills'

hateful miracle
strains fat.

He smiles:
the basset bounds.

He unsmiles: his face falls
but not in disappointment.

His head shows skull,
a study in bone,

honed to St. Jerome's
buzzkill pleasure.

He is wartime,
scorched earth,

his turf wasted
craters the generals' boys

die for. Its shrubs
inhale the smoke,

squirm for the sun,
root for fluid.

His eyes, the sentry's
lookout, look out:

he knows his face
is a trench afire.

He grins with all
his arrows of teeth,

he opens his mouth, he says
Stick out your tongue.

Clay's Face Is: Originally appeared in *Clay*,
Trio House Press, 2013.

JUANA M. RAMOS
[EL SALVADOR]

Juana M. Ramos was born in Santa Ana, El Salvador, and resides in New York where she teaches Spanish and Literature in York College, CUNY. She has collaborated with a variety of literary events. She has also participated in poetry festivals in Mexico, Colombia, Dominican Republic, Honduras, Cuba, Puerto Rico and Spain, among others. The first edition of her poetry collection *Multiplicada en mí* was published in NY in 2010 and a second revised and extended edition was released in 2014. Her poems and stories have been included in anthologies and literary journals (both printed and online) around the world.

Juana M. Ramos nació en Santa Ana, El Salvador y reside en la ciudad de Nueva York donde es profesora de español y literatura en York College, CUNY (La universidad pública de la Ciudad de Nueva York). Ha colaborado en la organización de diferentes eventos literarios y ha participado en festivales internacionales en México, Colombia, República Dominicana, Honduras, Cuba, Puerto Rico, El Salvador y España, entre otros. La primera edición de su poemario *Multiplicada en mí* se publicó en la ciudad de NY en junio de 2010 y en febrero de 2014 la segunda edición revisada y ampliada. Además, sus poemas y relatos han aparecido publicados en varias antologías, revistas literarias y digitales alrededor del mundo.

METRO

En la estación,
el tren de las nueve menos diez
aparece a tiempo
como todo en la ciudad,
imponente en la distancia,
cotidiano ya de cerca,
contrito al momento de abordarlo.
Se desplaza frío, calculador,
una voz monótona sin cara y sin nombre
predice las próximas paradas.
Cabezas inclinadas sumergidas
en las medias noticias que
ostentan los periódicos, voces
que tropiezan, criaturas inconformes
en coches que bloquean
las entradas , las salidas.
Cual río, un café derramado en el piso
se abre paso entre la gente.
Arboles, techos, cables de luz,
cúpulas, una tienda de disfraces
que se ofrece rebajada en un letrero,
un cementerio a lo lejos amanece
y se estira entre los vivos;
todos se conjugan atónitos
ante un tren que hiere el paisaje,
que parte y penetra la ciudad.

PEDRO ARTURO ESTRADA
[COLOMBIA]

Pedro Arturo Estrada (1956) is a Colombian poet, story teller and essayist. He has published the following books: *Poemas en blanco y negro* (1994); *Fatum* (2000); *Oscura edad* (2006); *Suma del tiempo* (2009); *Des/historias* (2012); *Poemas de Otra/parte* (2012); *Locus Solus* (2013) y *Blanco y Negro* (personal anthology) (2014). Among others, he received the Ciro Mendía and Casa Silva awards in 2004 and 2013 respectively. His work has been included in anthologies around the world.

Pedro Arturo Estrada –Poeta, narrador y ensayista colombiano, 1956. Ha publicado *Poemas en blanco y negro* (1994); *Fatum* (2000); *Oscura edad* (2006); *Suma del tiempo* (2009); *Des/historias* (2012); *Poemas de Otra/parte* (2012); *Locus Solus* (2013) y *Blanco y Negro* (Selección personal de textos) (2014). Es premio nacional Ciro Mendía en 2004, y Casa Silva, 2013, entre otros. Sus textos aparecen en diferentes antologías alrededor del mundo.

COUNTRY OF SILENCE

Someone dares to ask after him who has not returned.
And the shadows answer: nothing, nobody, no one.
Someone wanders sniffing the last steps,
the moans he left in the air, the voices that still
creep in under the doors. Someone
under the damp sheets of midnight
can't get to sleep, waits until the high
desolation of dawn for that news, that now, that enough,
that final cry which will reestablish the course of days
and unleash the voice over the void
dug by years of silence
and fear.

Translated by Laura Chalar

PAÍS DE SILENCIO

Alguien se atreve a preguntar por el que no ha
vuelto.
Y las sombras le contestan: nada, nadie, ninguno.
Alguien deambula husmeando los últimos pasos,
los ayes que dejó en el aire, las voces que aún
se cuelan por debajo de las puertas. Alguien
bajo las sábanas húmedas de la medianoche
no logra conciliar el sueño, espera hasta la alta
desolación del alba esa noticia, ese ya, ese basta,
ese grito final que restablezca el curso de los días
y desate la voz sobre el vacío
excavado por años de silencio
y miedo.

DANNIEL SCHOONEBEEK
[USA]

Daniel Schoonebeek's first book of poems, *American Barricade*, is out now from YesYes Books. A chapbook, *Family Album*, was published by Poor Claudia in 2013, and an EP of recorded poems, *Trench Mouth*, is available from Black Cake Records. His work has appeared in *Poetry, Tin House, Boston Review, Fence, BOMB, Indiana Review, jubilat, Denver Quarterly*, and elsewhere. He writes a column on poetry for *The American Reader;* hosts the Hatchet Job reading series, and edits the PEN Poetry Series. In 2015, Poor Claudia will release his second book, a travelogue called *C'est La Guerre.*

El primer libros de Danniel Schoonebeek *American Barricade* acaba de ser publicado por YesYes Books. La plaquette *Family Album* fue publicada por Poor Claudia en 2013. La publicación electrónica *Trench Mouth* está disponible en la página de Black Cake Records. Su trabajo ha aparecido en revistas como *Poetry, Tin House, Boston Review, Fence, BOMB, Indiana Review, jubilat, Denver Quarterly*. Escribe una columna sobre poesía para *The American Reader;* presenta la serie de lectura Hatchet Job y edita PEN Poetry Series. En 2015, Poor Claudia publicará su segundo libro, un texto de viajes llamado *C'est La Guerre.*

GENEALOGY

Men loyal first off to silence run in my family.
Ask about the women we say women.
What a scream. Ask about the men we say.
Men loyal only to stillness run in my family.
Not the same, you understand, as when a man.
Who refuses to budge withdraws into himself.
As when one wounds a tree to draw its sap.
Only to find the bucket come evening is empty.
Men of such stillness you hear us pulse.
Loyal to nothing like my father whose father.
Was a man who when he saw himself said.
I am too small. Too small within this world.
And too full of talk. My life I would live.
Could I live as a potato bug loves, beating.
Myself into the ground when I need you.
Then comes the sun and draws its cutlass.
And Opa's tongue the first off to silence.
Story I learned my father wouldn't tell me.
For though he was a man who couldn't read.
Music, he still found a way to write it, his life.
A short movement composed solely of rests.
Two sons he had two summers far too loud.
Now I am finished with my strings, he says.
Enough hammer, enough sustain, the end.
Men loyal first off to sustenance or sentence.
Ask about the women we say what women.
We have are women who have nothing.
There is my brother leading a horse whose.
Hunger is so loud it shakes the earth shakes.
The trees and when the apples fall he eats.
If she feeds he feeds her only from his knife.
If she rides he rides her only when he leaves.
There is me. Loyal only to when I tell myself.
That boy who has written across his wrist.
I'm god would make a good son but only if his.
Voice is a silence in which now I appear.
Ask about his mother he says mother.
Let her rip. Men who mean something.
Different than you when they say we.
Are loyal first off to the end, to the end.

From *American Barricade*, YesYesBooks, 2014

MARGARITA DRAGO
[ARGENTINA]

Margarita Drago is an Argentinean professor, poet and narrator who has lived in the USA since she was released from prison. As former political prisoner and writer, she has participated in conferences, colloquia, book fairs and poetry festivals in the USA, Argentina, Peru, Mexico, Honduras, El Salvador, Dominican Republic, Puerto Rico, Cuba, Spain and France. She is the author of the poetry collection *Con la memoria al ras de la garganta;* and the memoir *Fragmentos de la memoria: Recuerdos de una experiencia carcelaria (1975-1980)* translated as *Memory Tracks: Fragments from Prison (1975-1980).* Her work has appeared in literary journals in the USA and Latin America.

Margarita Drago, catedrática, poeta y narradora argentina radicada en Estados Unidos desde que salió de la cárcel. Como ex-prisionera política y escritora ha participado en congresos, coloquios, ferias del libro y festivales de poesía en los Estados Unidos, Argentina, Perú, México, Honduras, El Salvador, República Dominicana, Puerto Rico, Cuba, España y Francia. Es autora del poemario *Con la memoria al ras de la garganta; Fragmentos de la memoria: Recuerdos de una experiencia carcelaria (1975-1980); Memory Tracks: Fragments from Prison (1975-1980).* Sus poemas y relatos han aparecido en antologías y revistas literarias de Estados Unidos y América Latina.

SI DESAPARECIERA EL SUR

Si desapareciera el sur
perdería sentido la vida,
el norte me dio aposento,
no origen.

Si se desvaneciera la tristeza
de tus días grises
se derrumbaría el sustento
de mis días de gloria.

Si el olvido oscureciera
la memoria
de los cuerpos cautivos
se empañaría el recuerdo
de la luz.

Si el tiempo borrara
las huellas del infame
impresas en mi cuerpo,
sería mujer sin nombre,
sin pasado,
sin historia.

LEONARDO NIN
[R. DOMINICANA]

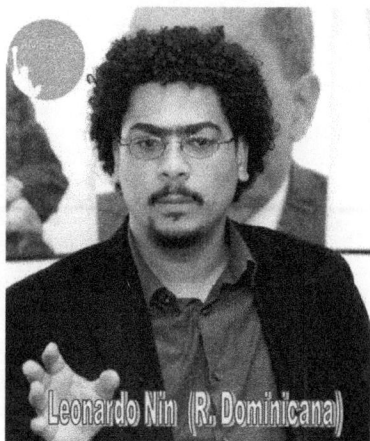

Leonardo Nin: Dominican anthropologist and writer, graduated from Harvard University. He is one of the main representative of the Dominican Diaspora Literature Movement. He has published several books of short stories, which include *Guazábaras* and *Sacrileges of the excommunicated*. Also the collection of poems *Paid Space* and the novels *I only know that they called her Shadow* and *Tomorrow, when God dies*. His literary work and his essays on linguistic and anthropological research have been published in various journals and anthologies in the United States, Latin America and Europe.

Leonardo Nin: Antropólogo y escritor dominicano, egresado de la universidad de Harvard. Es uno de los principales representantes de la literatura dominicana de la Diáspora. Ha publicado varios libros de cuentos, entre los que figuran: *Guazábaras y Sacrilegios del excomulgado*. También el poemario *Espacio pagado* y las novelas *Sólo sé que le llamaban Sombra* y *Mañana, si Dios muere*. Sus trabajos de investigación lingüística y literaria han sido publicados en diversas revistas y antologías en los Estados Unidos, Latinoamérica y Europa.

ADDENDUM I

This poem is an eternal past,
ephemeral epitaph
rough memory of a satrap
between two mirrors.
This poem is a fallible
and morbid introspection,
cynical vomit of alphabet,
cradled song of a beast
juxtaposing a body
between two abysses.

If my hand was made out of ink
I would had tattooed my story
in the empty walls of oblivion.
I'm a black shadow, invented notion,
illegible testimony of a superfluous
scream breaking the silent of the night.

I invented thousands of lands to be prophet:
distinguished award of an idiot.
I erected mountains to become echo,
perennial skeleton of a fool.
I cried, stamping my voice
in the scattered winds of time,
tenuous dreams in shroud of memories.
Now,
I'm only an improper attachment
to a will
buried in a walking body.

ADDENDUM I

Este poema es un pasado sempiterno
epitafio efímero
burda memoria de un sátrapa
entre dos espejos.
Este poema es falible introspección del morbo,
cínico vómito de alfabeto,
canción de cuna para una bestia
yuxtaponiendo un cuerpo
entre dos abismos.

Si mi mano fuera de tinta
tatuaría mi historia en la pared del olvido,
sombra negra, noción inventada,
testimonio ilegible de un diario superfluo
en la quejumbre silente de una sombra en noche.

Inventé mil tierras para ser profeta,
insigne galardón de idiota.
Erigí montañas para hacerme eco,
perenne esqueleto de fatuo.
Grité, estampando mi voz
en el cuero de un viento desvencijado
en el tiempo,
tenue sepultura de sueños en mortaja de memorias.
Ahora, soy anexo impropio a un testamento
sepultado en un cuerpo.

ALEX LIMA
[ECUADOR]

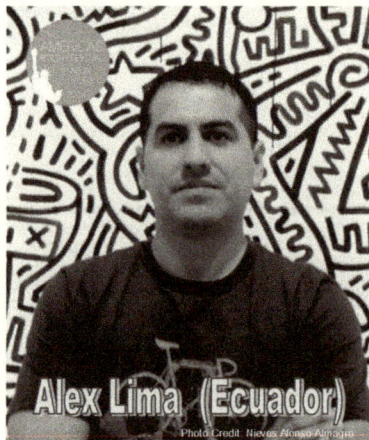

Alex Lima (Ecuador) is the author of two poetry collections *Inverano* (2008) and *Bilocaciones* (2011). He is also co-founder of *Entre Rascacielos*, Epsilon Kappa's journal of creative writing at St. John's University. He has served as editor of *Hybrido magazine,* and is currently an active member of the art collective *We Are You Project*. Mr. Lima is co-founder of the Latino Arts Council of Long Island, a non-profit organization aimed at promoting inter-cultural dialogue and literacy through the arts. He recently completed his doctoral dissertation on 18th-century poetry of the Americas at The Graduate Center (CUNY).

Alex Lima (Ecuador) es autor de dos libros de poemas *Inverano* (2008) y *Bilocaciones* (2011), es cofundador de *Entre Rascacielos* la revista de escritura creativa de Epsilon Kappa en St. John's University. Ha trabajado como editor de *Hybrido magazine* y en la actualidad es miembro activo del colectivo *We Are You Project*. Es cofundador de Latino Arts Council of Long Island, una organización sin ánimo de lucro que promueve el diálogo intercultural a través de las artes. Recientemente terminó su disertación doctoral sobre poesía del siglo 18 en las Américas en The Graduate Center (CUNY).

RUFO

A roof is not a rooftop
It's a tar oasis in the middle of a concrete desert
It's the summer terrace in the midst of a heat wave
It's the backyard for those kids who have no backyard
It's the dance floor where salsa moves are improvised
With music from a boom box and a can of Budweiser
Where the compai from Mayagüez in his tank-top and beret
Fakes a full turn like a Welterweight boxer
To put his virtues on display... like he is about to sit on air.

A rufo is not a rooftop
It's a meeting place for lovers
Where daddy's girl meets her boo,
It's neutral territory where negotiations
about the future of our neighborhood take place,
The day when Ecuadorian girls shall play with
Polish girls, walking, holding hands down
Manhattan Avenue to McCarren Park,
To enjoy a picnic with sausage, coquito, and tostones
As they lay on the grass next to the trash can,
Half-green, half-rusty.

A rufo is not a rooftop
It's the storage place for things no longer needed in the house. Well!
It isn't really a house, a wagon apartment rather,
With no entryways, one enters through the kitchen and exits
through someone else's bedroom, where the concept of privacy
is non-existent since there is no room for secrets.

A rufo is not a rooftop
It's an appendix to the home where every-day life
unrolls, with a barbecue, an unreturned bike, a drying line,
A vintage point from where the other city can be seen,
Framed, like the Imagists insisted, between the chimney
and the water tank.

ROOF

Un rufo no es un techo
es un oasis de alquitrán en medio del desierto de concreto
es la terraza estival en los calores de verano
es el dominio donde juegan los niños que no tienen patio
es la pista de baile donde se improvisa una salsita
con radio boombox y Budweiser de lata
donde el compai de Mayagüez con boina y bividí
amaga con dar una vuelta cual boxeador peso Welter
pa' demostrar sus virtudes al girar… como que se sienta.

Un rufo no es un techo
es el lugar de encuentro de los enamorados,
donde la niña de papi puede verse con su jebo,
es el lugar neutral donde se realizan las negociaciones
de lo que será el futuro de nuestro vecindario, cuando las
niñas polacas podrán jugar con las niñas ecuatorianas
y se irán caminando de la mano por Manhattan Avenue
hasta el parque McCarren,
para hacer un picnic con salchicha, coquito y tostones
y tirarse al césped seco junto al zafacón medio verde,
medio pelao.

Un rufo no es un techo
es el trastero de las cosas que no caben dentro de casa. ¡Bueno!
eso de "casa" es un decir, del apartamento en forma de vagón
sin puertas, donde se entra por la cocina y se sale por
recámara ajena, donde la privacidad no existe porque
ya no queda hueco donde esconder los secretos.

Un rufo no es un techo
es un apéndice de la casa donde también se hace vida,
con barbacoa, bicicletas ajenas y ropa tendida,
desde donde se divisa la otra ciudad, enmarcada
al estilo imaginista, entre la chimenea y el tanque de agua.

JULIET P. HOWARD
[USA]

JP HOWARD akaJuliet P. Howard is a poet, Cave Canem graduate fellow, member of The Hot Poets Collective and native New Yorker. She curates and nurtures Women Writers in Bloom Poetry Salon (WWBPS), a forum offering women writers at all levels a venue to come together in a positive and supportive space. WWBPS hosts monthly literary Salons in NY. JP's debut collection of poetry is forthcoming from The Operating System. JP is a VONA/Voices 2014 Alum. She is a Lambda Literary Foundation Emerging LGBT Voices Fellow, as well as a Cave Canem Fellow in Residence at the Virginia Center for the Creative Arts. She was a finalist for Astraea's Lesbian Writers Fund for poetry. Her poems have been published in: *Adrienne: A Poetry Journal of Queer Women, The Best American Poetry Blog, MiPOesias, African Voices Magazine, Kweli Journal, The Mom Egg, "Of Fire, Of Iron", Talking Writing, Muzzle Magazine, Connotation Press, TORCH, Queer Convention: A Chapbook of Fierce, Cave Canem Anthology XII: Poems 2008-2009, Promethean Literary Journal* and *Poetry in Performance.* She was awarded an MFA in Creative Writing from the City College of New York in 2009 and holds a BA from Barnard College. Salon Facebook page: https://www.facebook.com/WomenWritersin-Bloom.PoetrySalon

JP HOWARD también conocida como Juliet P. Howard es poeta, becaria graduada de Cave Canem, miembro de The Hot Poets Collective y neoyorquina. Ella cura y alimenta el Women Writers in Bloom Poetry Salon (WWBPS), un foro que ofrece a las escritoras de todos los niveles un espacio positivo y acogedor para reunirse. WWBPS organiza salones literarios en

Nueva York. Su primera colección de será publicada por The Operating System. JP es exalumna del VONA/Voices 2014. Ha sido becaria de Lambda Literary Foundation Emerging LGBT Voices y becaria residente del Cave Canem Fellow en el Virginia Center for the Creative Arts. Fue finalista en el Astraea's Lesbian Writers Fund for poetry. Sus poemas han sido publicados en *Adrienne: A Poetry Journal of Queer Women, The Best American Poetry Blog, MiPOesias, African Voices Magazine, Kweli Journal, The Mom Egg, "Of Fire, Of Iron", Talking Writing, Muzzle Magazine, Connotation Press, TORCH, Queer Convention: A Chapbook of Fierce, Cave Canem Anthology XII: Poems 2008-2009, Promethean Literary Journal* y *Poetry in Performance.* En 2009 recibió un MFA en escritura creative de The City College of New York y un pregrado de Barnard College. La página de Face Book del salón literario es https://www.facebook.com/WomenWritersinBloom.PoetrySalon

PRAISE OUR MAMAS

Praise our Mamas
Praise the ones who loved us fiercely
Praise Mamas who left us behind
Praise their bosoms
Praise tears we shed all those years
Praise softness of skin against skin
Praise therapists who listened again and again
Praise poems we birthed
Praise our ability to forgive
Praise the poet's tears,
each time she relived childhood memories
Praise that sweet child that lives on
Praise her soft voice
Praise Mama humming your favorite lullaby
Praise Mamas who shut the door
Praise Mamas whose doors were wide open
Praise "Come here sit on Mama lap baby" Mamas
Praise Mamas who never learned to look beyond their reflection
Praise Mama's reflection
Praise Mama in your mirror

Praise love's complicated contours
Praise her edges, sharp then soft
Praise Mamas who bend and open to hugs
Praise Mamas who never learned to hug
Praise a laying on of hands, soft like Mama's
Praise your best friend, who nurtures like a Mama
Praise the memory of Mama
Praise that soft spot in your heart
Name her Mama.

María Socorro Soto Alanís
[México]

María Socorro Soto Alanís. was born in Durango, Mexico. She studied engineering at Tecnológico de Durango and Political Science at Universidad Nacional Autónoma de México. She has received certificates in literature, philosophy and economy. She has written five books: *En estos días, Desnuda en el Viento, Fin de Milenio,En el día tercero se hizo el agua, Un mediodía de enero, Sor Juana: Virgen guerrera y Cuentos del Norte.* Her work has been included in newspapers and magazines in Mexico. She was a founding member of the cultural magazines *Revuelta* and *Cordillera*. Recently, she has served as president of the Writers Association of Durango A.C. She was also the deputy director of Casa de la Cultura, Historical Archives and Social Development Secretary of Durango. She has taught at Instituto Tecnológico de Durango.

María Socorro Soto Alanís. Nació en Durango, México. Estudió ingeniería en el Tecnológico de Durango y ciencias políticas en la Universidad Nacional Autónoma de México. Diplomada en literatura, historia, filosofía y economía. Ha publicado: *En estos días, Desnuda en el Viento, Fin de Milenio,En el día tercero se hizo el agua, Un mediodía de enero, Sor Juana: Virgen guerrera y Cuentos del Norte.* Ha publicado en periódicos y revistas nacionales. Fundadora de las revistas culturales *Revuelta y Cordillera*. Recientemente, fue presidente de la Sociedad de Escritores de Durango A.C. En Durango ha sido subdirectora de la Casa de la Cultura, del Archivo Histórico y en la Secretaría de Desarrollo Social. Fue catedrática en el Instituto Tecnológico de Durango.

80 MIL

Ochenta mil cruces
Madera de brazos tristes
Tierra que llora
Hijos sin volver
en un país de olvido.

Ochenta mil cuerpos abatidos
Noche que no termina
Plazas desoladas
donde el quiosco llora.
Campanas de lamento
Réquiem eterno.

Ochenta mil heridas
Llagas de la patria
Insomnio interminable
que moja las sábanas de llanto.

Ochenta mil lágrimas
Rosario de agua salada
Rostros que envejecen
en medio de patios olvidados
tristes por la ausencia.
Ochenta mil soledades
Cada quien la suya.

80 THOUSAND

Eighty thousand crosses
Wood of sad arms
Land that cries
Children without return
in a country of the forgotten.

Eighty thousand abated bodies
Endless night
Desolate plazas
where the kiosk cries.
Bells of lament
Eternal requiem.

Eighty thousand wounds
Patriotic gashes
Interminable insomnia
that wets the sheets with crying.

Eighty thousand tears
Salt water rosary
Aging faces
amidst forgotten yards
saddened by absence.
Eighty thousand solitudes
To each his own.

Translated by Pilar Gonzalez

MIGUEL FALQUEZ-CERTAIN
[COLOMBIA-USA]

Miguel Falquez-Certain (Barranquilla, Colombia) has been living in New York City for almost four decades, where he works as a multilingual translator and writer. He is the author of six volumes of poetry:*Reflejos de una máscara, Habitación en la palabra, Proemas en cámara ardiente, Doble corona, Usurpaciones y deicidios*, and *Palimpsestos*; of a short novel, *Bajo el adoquín, la playa*; of six plays: *La pasión, Moves Meet Metes Move: A Tragic Farce*, "Castillos de arena," "Allá en el club hay un runrún," "Una angustia se abre paso entre los huesos," and *Quemar las naves*, as well as of short stories and essays. Book Press–New York published *Triacas* (short fiction) and *Mañanayer* (poetry) in 2010. *Mañanayer* received the only honorable mention in The 2011 International Latino Book Awards in the category of Best Poetry Book – Spanish or Bilingual. He has participated in book fairs in Miami, Santo Domingo, New York, and Bogotá, and he has been a guest poet at literary conferences and festivals in Ecuador and the U.S.A. He translated both screenplays for Steven Soderbergh's Che Guevara biopics, *The Argentine* and *Guerrilla*. He is a member of PEN American Center, The American Translators Association, and Proz.com.

Miguel Falquez-Certain nació en Barranquilla (Colombia). Ha publicado cuentos, poemas, piezas de teatro, ensayos, traducciones y críticas literarias, teatrales y cinematográficas en Europa, Latinoamérica y los EE.UU. Su obra poética, dramática y narrativa ha sido distinguida con numerosos galardones. Licenciado en literaturas hispánica y francesa (Hunter College), 1980. Cursó estudios de doctorado en literatura comparada en New York University (1981-1985). Es autor de los poemarios *Reflejos de una máscara, Habitación en la palabra, Proemas en cámara ardiente, Doble corona, Usurpaciones y deicidios* y *Palimpsestos*; y de la novela corta *Bajo el adoquín, la playa* (Bucaramanga: Sic Editorial, 2004). En 2010, Book Press–New York publicó *Triacas* (compilación de su narrativa breve), así como *Mañanayer* (compilación de sus seis poemarios), libro que obtuvo la única mención honorífica en el *Latino Book Awards* en 2011 en la categoría de volumen de poesía en español. Ha participado en las Ferias del Libro de Bogotá, Miami, Santo Domingo y Nueva York, así como poeta invitado en congresos y festivales del Ecuador y de los Estados Unidos. Miembro de PEN American Center, American Translators Association y Proz.com. Vive en Nueva York desde hace más de siete lustros donde se desempeña como traductor en cinco idiomas.

THE NAME OF THINGS

There is always something that doesn't work with the reality of things.
If you look at the sunset and don't understand the journey which you are
About to undertake, it may be necessary to retrace your steps,
Perhaps to remember how the sky used to dip into the ocean
Like a deranged octopus's indomitable ink. Today, you don't feel
In your memory the muffled cry of disturbance or the reflux of
A secret gift: You understand the multiplicity of voices
And the unrelenting flow of your juices -either you jump or die
Or live or succeed, but the world carries on, aloof in its
Abysmal proximity, with the echoes of manifold offerings
And the abdications of dog days on the climax of death rattles,
Or, perhaps, with the unintelligible, sullen wailing that makes possible,
At long last, the historical knowledge of your reality.
It's possible to interpret and reinterpret each and every fact
In dissimilar ways, since we must know
What reason is and how to achieve it: Existence subverts
The truth, hiding it, displacing it, eliminating it.
Nonetheless, you don't understand the meticulousness of their
Performance -that eradicable ritual of their silent eloquence-
Or the struggle between competing meanings.
The world

Occupies the spaces of the mind: My genuine self,
I cannot possess, because reality is present
In transition. We are alone. In the midst of the absolute
Freedom of the night, in the resolute gesture of dispossession,
In the forgotten absence of ties, fetishes, and lineages,
In the glacial fire of the sunglows, dawn heralds
The unstoppable close of our drawn-out night and the onset of peace.

From *Work in Progress*

EL NOMBRE DE LAS COSAS

Siempre existe algo que no marcha con la realidad de las cosas.
Si miras el ocaso y no comprendes el viaje que a punto estás
de emprender, tal vez sea necesario recoger tus pasos,
acaso recordar cómo era el cielo que se sumergía en el océano
como la tinta indómita de un pulpo desquiciado. No sientes
hoy en el recuerdo el grito ahogado del disturbio ni el reflujo
de un don inconfeso: comprendes la pluralidad de voces
y la marcha indefectible de tus jugos, o saltas o mueres
o vives o triunfas, pero el mundo allí continúa, ajeno en su
cercanía de abismos, con los ecos de múltiples ofertas
y las renuncias de canículas en los estertores de la cúspide,
o tal vez con el llanto incomprensible y hosco que hace posible,
finalmente, el conocimiento histórico de tu realidad.
Cada hecho es posible interpretarlo y reinterpretarlo
de múltiples maneras, porque es necesario que sepamos
lo que es la razón y cómo alcanzarla: la existencia subvierte
la verdad, ocultándola, desplazándola, suprimiéndola.
Sin embargo, no comprendes la acuciosidad de sus
desempeños (ese rito inveterado de su muda elocuencia)
ni los conflictos de los diversos significados.
El mundo
ocupa los espacios de la mente: mi auténtico yo,
no puedo poseerlo, porque la realidad es presente
como transición. Estamos solos. En medio de la libertad

absoluta de la noche, en el gesto decidido de la desposesión,
en la ausencia irrecordable de ataduras, fetiches y estirpes,
el alba anuncia, en el incendio glacial de los arreboles,
el fin ineludible de nuestra larga noche y el inicio de la paz.

De *Obra en curso*

MARIELA DREYFUS
[PERÚ]

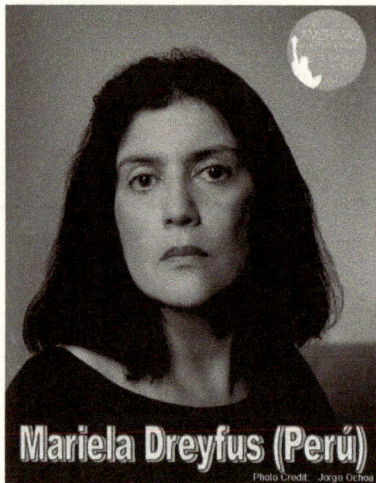

Mariela Dreyfus (Perú) has resided in New York since 1989. She has written the poetry collections: *Memorias de Electra* (Lima, 1984), *Placer fantasma* (Premio Asociación Peruano-Japonesa, Lima, 1993), *Ónix* (Lima, 2001), *Pez* (Lima, 2005) / *Pez/Fish* (New Delhi, 2014), *Morir es un arte* (Lima, 2010) and *Cuaderno músico* (2014). Her poetry has been translated to English, French and Portuguese. It has also been included in numerous anthologies of Peruvian and Latin American poetry such as *Invencible del amor la fortaleza. Once poetas iberoamericanas en Nueva York* (Nueva York, 2011), *Espléndida iracundia. Antología consultada de la poesía peruana. 1968-2008* (Lima, 2012) and *Kloaka. Antología poética* (Madrid, 2014). Dreyfus is the author of *Soberanía y transgresión: César Moro* (Lima, 2008), and co-editor of the critical volumes *Nadie sabe mis cosas. Reflexiones en torno a la poesía de Blanca Varela* (Lima, 2007) and *Esta mística de relatar cosas sucias. Ensayos en torno a la obra de Carmen Ollé* (Lima, 2014). She cofounded the Kloaka poetic movement (1982-1984). She received a Ph.D. in Hispanic American Literature from Columbia University and is currently a professor in the Masters program in Creative Writing in Spanish at NYU.

Mariela Dreyfus (Perú) reside en Nueva York desde 1989. Ha escrito los poemarios *Memorias de Electra* (Lima, 1984), *Placer fantasma* (Premio Asociación Peruano-Japonesa, Lima, 1993), *Ónix* (Lima, 2001), *Pez* (Lima, 2005) / *Pez/Fish* (New Delhi, 2014), *Morir es un arte*(Lima, 2010) y *Cuaderno músico* (2014). Su poesía ha sido traducida al inglés, francés y portugués, y se incluye en numerosas antologías de poesía peruana y latinoamericana, entre otras: *Invencible del amor la fortaleza. Once poetas iberoamericanas en Nueva York* (Nueva York, 2011), *Espléndida iracundia. Antología consultada de la poesía peruana. 1968-2008* (Lima, 2012) y *Kloaka. Antología poética* (Madrid, 2014). Dreyfus es autora del estudio *Soberanía y transgresión: César Moro* (Lima, 2008), y co-editora de los volúmenes críticos *Nadie sabe mis cosas. Reflexiones en torno a la poesía de Blanca Varela* (Lima, 2007) y *Esta mística de relatar cosas sucias. Ensayos en torno a la obra de Carmen Ollé* (Lima, 2014). Fundadora del movimiento poético Kloaka (1982-1984). Doctora en Literatura Hispanoamericana por la Universidad de Columbia, actualmente es profesora en la Maestría de Escritura Creativa en Español de la Universidad de Nueva York.

WHO BRINGS FORTH THE RAIN?

Pina Bausch)

This is a dance you and I
we travel together like clams
like black goose barnacles attached
to the largest most precarious rock
our existence depends solely upon
the next step we take over this oily surface
only our back our plexus our sex the mist
joins us together our arms are vanes
our lips inhale this energy as intense
as velocity the same space over time and
over you and over me the hours flow and
space contracts because I coil
myself around your waist or you repose
on my chest and then slide off
toward my belly and at that spot I
make a circle tie you to my lap
and the landscape is black the waters
swirl and in this whirlpool
you strip me of my clothes I
strip myself of modesty we are

two newborn amphibians
dragging a tail that suddenly
becomes a wing lifting us up and over the crag
a guttural sound like a bird
a croak like a wounded raven
identifies you defines me and it rains
in great buckets very cold the water
grazes us and caresses perhaps it boils but
it doesn't matter neither you nor I let ourselves
fall except into this innocent passion
harmless like when I cover your
eyes and tell you to follow the line down
my nape stop at the fissure of the first
vertebrae feel the ribbon that ties
my body and in one two or three infinite
seconds I will turn around in order to
show you my breasts the dark nipple
that gets you worked up and then perhaps
the rain will fall again and a joyful
music will make the rhythm descend down to my legs
I will perform a plié adjusting you to my pelvis and
you rising a few centimeters will
caress my fissure but we will not stop
advancing on the path as though a thread
from above pulls us and we
might ask where it comes from who
is the demiurge that brings forth so much water
from the heavens while we
continue croaking and your body and my
body invent anew a pirouette
and this time from the vertex of my eye I see
your shadow stalking me from behind
sufficiently skillful to climb with our
batrachian feet up to a summit that shines
like the heavenly vault but we can't see
beyond the warm strands of your hair
of my hair face down I splash you I distance myself
barely three inches three minutes to dance
in front of you seduce or satiate you while you
also do not abandon the movement rather you

applaud me you sway your hips and in that instant
your torso already nude feels my embrace and at that
moment when we don't know if the sun is about to leave
or return tomorrow or if there will even be a tomorrow in
this story in which I want to stop fix
our image as lovely limpets some
mollusk would need to define our desire
to walk like this side by side the world never so near
nor so far that my heart will shrink
from not finding you in you I have found the perfect
coupling of bodies the couplet that I sing to you
when the drizzle worsens and this unique
heraldic copula of ours the shield that frees us
from all tedium damp in the time of ardent love.

Translated by Gabriel Amor

¿QUIÉN HACE BROTAR LA LLUVIA?

(*Pina Bausch*)

ésta es una danza tú y yo
viajamos unidos como almejas
como percebes negros pegados
a la roca más grande más precaria
nuestra existencia sólo depende
del paso que daremos sobre esta
superficie aceitosa sólo la espalda
el plexo el sexo un vaho acuático
nos liga los brazos son aspas
los labios aspiran esta energía
que es tan intensa como velocidad
igual espacio sobre tiempo y sobre
ti y sobre mí las horas fluyen y
el espacio se acorta porque yo
me enrosco a tu cintura o tú reposas
en mi pecho y luego te deslizas

hacia el vientre y allí mismo yo
hago un círculo te ato a mi regazo
y es negro el paisaje las aguas
se revuelven y en ese remolino
tú me despojas de mi traje yo
me despojo del pudor somos
dos anfibios recién nacidos
arrastrando una cola que de pronto
es un ala nos eleva y sobre el peñasco
un sonido gutural como de ave
un croar de cuervo herido te
identifica me define y llueve a grandes
baldazos con gran frío el agua
nos roza y acaricia acaso hierve pero
no importa ni tú ni yo nos dejamos
caer salvo en esta inocente pasión
inofensiva como cuando te cubro
los ojos y te digo sigue la línea que baja
por mi nuca detente en la fisura de las
primeras vértebras palpa la cinta que ata
mi corpiño y en uno dos o tres segundos
infinitos yo me daré la vuelta y he de
mostrarte mis senos el oscuro pezón
que te arrebata y entonces tal vez caiga
de nuevo lluvia y una música alegre hará
que el ritmo descienda hasta las piernas
yo haré un plié ajustándote a mi pelvis y
tú elevándote unos centímetros irás
acariciando mi hendidura pero no dejaremos
de avanzar sobre la pista como si un hilo
desde arriba nos moviera y entonces uno
podría preguntarse de dónde viene quién
es el demiurgo que hace brotar tanta agua
desde el firmamento mientras nosotros
continuamos croando y tu cuerpo y mi
cuerpo inventan de nuevo una pirueta
y esta vez desde el vértice del ojo veo
tu sombra que por detrás me acecha
con la soltura suficiente para trepar con
nuestros pies batracios hasta una cúspide

que luce como la bóveda celeste pero no
se ve más que las tibias hebras de tu cabello
de mi cabello boca abajo te salpico me alejo
apenas tres pulgadas tres minutos para danzar
frente a ti seducirte o saciarte mientras tú
tampoco abandonas el movimiento más bien
aplaudes cimbreas las caderas y en ese instante
tu torso ya desnudo siente mi abrazo y a esa
hora en que no sabemos si el sol está por irse
o volverá mañana o si acaso hay mañana en
esta historia donde yo quiero detenerme fijar
nuestra imagen de lapas adoradas nuestro deseo
de andar así de a dos el mundo nunca tan cerca
ni tampoco tan lejos que se me encoja el corazón
de no encontrarte en ti he hallado el perfecto
acoplarse de los cuerpos la copla que te canto
cuando la llovizna se acelera y es esta cópula
nuestra única heráldica el escudo que nos libra
de todo tedio húmedos en el tiempo ardiente amor.

ISABEL ESPINAL
[USA]

Isabel Espinal was born in New York City in 1964, two years after her parents immigrated from the Cibao countryside in the Dominican Republic. She attended MIT and graduated from Princeton University with a degree in Romance Languages and Literature. She earned a Masters degree in Library and Information Studies from UC Berkeley in 1991 and has been a librarian ever since. She also gave birth to and raised three children, now 21, 19 and 17 years old. In 1993, inspired by feelings of life and mortality inherent in being a mother, Isabel started writing down poetry. She published a chapbook of poetry, *Clean Sheets*, in 1996, as part of a series edited by poet Lourdes Vazquez, and in anthologies such as *Tertuliando / Hanging Out* and an issue of the journal *Callaloo* dedicated to Dominican Literature. Isabel also has translated poetry and prose, in particular the poetry of Yrene Santos. Isabel currently works fulltime as a librarian while pursuing a PhD in American Studies with a dissertation on contemporary Dominican women writers in the United States. In 2013-2014 she was President of REFORMA: The National Association to Promote Library and Information Services to Latinos and the Spanish Speaking.

Isabel Espinal nació en Nueva York en 1964, dos años después de que sus padres inmigraran desde la región de El Cibao en la República Dominicana. Asistió a MIT y se graduó de la universidad de Princeton del programa de Lenguas Romances y Literatura. Recibió una maestría en bibliotecología y estudios de la información de UC Berkeley en 1991 y ha sido bibliotecaria desde entonces. Tiene tres hijos de 21, 19 y 17 años. En 1993, inspirada por los sentimientos de mortalidad inherentes a la maternidad, comenzó a escribir poesía. Publicó una plaquette *Clean Sheets* (1996) como parte de la serie editada por la poeta Lourdes Vázquez y en antologías como *Tertuliando / Hanging Out* y un número de la revista *Callaloo* dedicado a la literatura dominicana. También ha traducido prosa y poesía, en particular la obra de la poeta Yrene Santos. En la actualidad trabaja en una biblioteca y termina estudios de doctorado con una disertación sobre las escritoras dominicanas contemporáneas en USA. En 2013-14 fue presidente de RE-FORMA una asociación nacional para promover los servicios de biblioteca e información para los latinos y los hispanohablantes.

Wake up and smell

That year she started sleeping
    with poetry.
At first just sleeping–
    they didn't fuck
    or hardly touch–
just getting into
    each other's dreams.
They were both tired
    from using up the world
    from being used up.
Then one night she took him
    into her hands
    into her sex
and the quiet plum inside her
    burst open with verses
and the words came
    dripping down her legs.
What no one ever wrote before
    is that it wasn't just that night
but also the next morning
    as she drank her coffee,
then on the train, then during her meetings,
    the sticky smell rose up
because the words kept dripping,
    dripping.

KEISHA-GAYE ANDERSON
[JAMAICA-USA]

Keisha-Gaye Anderson is a Jamaican-born poet, creative writer, and screenwriter. She is the author of a forthcoming collection of poetry titled *Gathering the Waters* (Jamii Publishing, December 2014). Her writing has appeared in a number of collections, anthologies, and literary magazines, including *Renaissance Noire, The Killens Review of Arts and Letters, Small Axe Salon, Streetnotes: Cross Cultural Poetics, African Voices Magazine, Mosaic Literary Magazine, Captured by the City: Perspectives on Urban Culture, Poems on the Road to Peace: A Collective Tribute to Dr. King, Sometimes Rhythm, Sometimes Blues: Young African Americans on Love, Relationships, Sex, and the Search for Mr. Right,* the *Mom Egg, Caribbean in Transit Arts Journal, Women Writers in Bloom Poetry Salon* blog, *and Bet on Black: African American Women Celebrate Fatherhood in the Age of Barak Obama*. Keisha is also a founding poet of Poets for Ayiti. Keisha holds a B.A. from Syracuse University's Newhouse School and College of Arts and Science and an M.F.A. in Creative Writing from The City College, CUNY. For the past ten years, Keisha has worked as a higher education communications and marketing manager. She lives in Brooklyn, NY with her husband and two children.
Learn more about Keisha at www.keishagaye.com.

Keisha-Gaye Anderson nació en Jamaica, es poeta, escritora creativa y guionista. Es autora de la colección de poesía de próxima aparición *Gathering the Waters* (Jamii Publishing, Diciembre 2014). Sus escritos han aparecido en colecciones, antología y revistas como *Renaissance Noire, The Killens Review of Arts and Letters, Small Axe Salon, Streetnotes: Cross Cultural*

Poetics, African Voices Magazine, Mosaic Literary Magazine, Captured by the City: Perspectives on Urban Culture, Poems on the Road to Peace: A Collective Tribute to Dr. King, Sometimes Rhythm, Sometimes Blues: Young African Americans on Love, Relationships, Sex, and the Search for Mr. Right, the *Mom Egg, Caribbean in Transit Arts Journal, Women Writers in Bloom Poetry Salon* blog y *Bet on Black: African American Women Celebrate Fatherhood in the Age of Barak Obama.* También es fundadora de Poets for Ayiti.
Keisha recibió un pregrado de la Universidad de Syracuse en el Newhouse School and College of Arts and Science y una maestría en escritura creativa de The City College, CUNY. Desde diez años, ha trabajado como administradora de mercadeo y comunicaciones en educación superior. Vive en Brooklyn con su esposo y sus dos hijos.

ANCESTORS

Well…
you wanted to look
into the dark,
didn't you?

So, don't curse these eyes
We gave them to you

And sent you to
straighten the bends in
these steel tracks
that link all our names
rusted under salt water
buried beneath bundles
of cane

Sing songs into candle flame
for these bones of mine
that now reach through you
stand you into
six feet of woman

They have not forgotten how to
brace against the lash
and bend backward
for the bembe

Each day
We move with you
can't you hear?

We are riding the rhythm
that beats these words
through your center

You beg us to enter
but We never left
We is Me
is You
is Us all now
together
since forever

We laugh
and lift
your sight toward
sea shells
star shine
sleeping poetry
in every alley
and pissed on corner

We tune your ears
to the footfall of predators
who clutch your breasts
in the blindness of their thoughts
stroke their loneliness
to the bow line of your lips

You wanted to know
not believe

So see it all here
now
be Our telescope
and chart the course
to home

Build a ladder
with these visions
that lift Us up
one by one
hand over hand
after-birth
to under dirt

We listen with you
roll slow up
this mountain
that needed us to tumble down
break ground
move things

So, look here:
Kill your fear
open these eyes
pull Us back together
march us home

JOSÉ MIGUEL DE LA ROSA
[R. DOMINICANA]

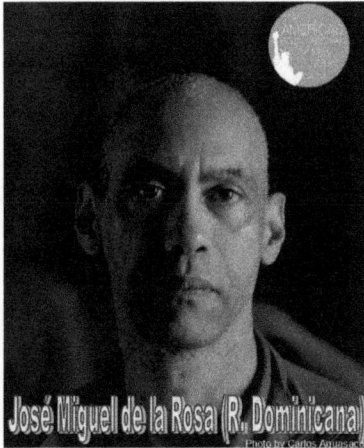

José Miguel de la Rosa was born in Santo Domingo, Dominican Republic. The studied Latin American Literature at The City College of New York (CUNY). He was a member of the literary group Pensum.He is also a co-founder of the Hispano/Latino Cultural Center of New York (HLCCNY). He has published the poetry collections *Entre sonrisas y sueños* and *Otra latidud.* Some of his works have been included in anthologies such as *Niveles del imán, La espiga del siglo, Tertuliando, Historias de Washington Heights y otros rincones del mundo, Viajeros del rocío, Noches de vino y rosas (Obsidiana Press, 2010.), Campo de los patos (Oviedo, Espana, 2013), Festival Latinoamericano de Poesia Ciudad de Nueva York 2012: antología (Urpi Editores/Academia Norteamericana de la Lengua, 2012).* He has also published the play *La loca de la estación Central (Micielo Ediciones, México, 2010).*

José Miguel de la Rosa nació en Santo Domingo, República Dominicana. Estudió literatura hispanoamericana en City College (CUNY). Fue miembro del grupo literario Pensum. Es co-fundador del Hispano/Latino Cultural Center de la Ciudad de Nueva York (HLCCNY). Ha publicado los poemarios: *Entre sonrisas y sueños* & *Otra latitud.* Algunos de sus trabajos aparecen en las siguientes antologías: *Niveles del imán, La espiga del siglo, Tertuliando, Historias de Washington Heights y otros rincones del mundo, Viajeros del rocío, Noches de vino y rosas (Obsidiana Press, 2010.), Campo de los patos (Oviedo, Espana, 2013), Festival Latinoamericano de Poesia Ciudad de Nueva York 2012: antología (Urpi Editores/Academia Norteamericana de la Lengua, 2012).* Tiene una obra de un acto publicada, *La loca de la estación Central (Micielo Ediciones, México, 2010).*

VIAJE

Sentir el azul como un golpe que ciega
Sembrar olvidos para que crezcan flores
sobre los rieles el tren pasa y se aleja
ansia ojos humo espesura
esparadrapos sabe Dios de qué herida
un barrio con nubes rotas por el desprecio de santos que se han ido
aquí solo se suben cuestas que hacen sudar la gota gorda
y la vida
pero aun hay pájaros que se posan en árboles con retoño
juegos que inventar en esta plaza
a esta hora en que solos los faroles duermen
aridez alambres hierros nubes es solo el paisaje
y un rastro de grafitti en el tiempo

WINSTON MORALES CHAVARRO
[COLOMBIA]

Winston Morales Chavarro was born in Neiva-Huila (Colombia), 1969. He is a social communicator and journalist and holds an MA in Cultural Studies with a concentration in Hispanic American Literature from Universidad Andina Simón Bolívar, Quito. He has won numerous literary awards, among them Concurso Nacional de Poesía Universidad de Antioquia (2001). Some of his poems have been translated to English, French, Portuguese and Italian. He has published the following poetry collections: *Aniquirona*- Trilce Editores 1998; *La Lluvia y el ángel* (Coautoría)-Trilce Editores 1999; *De Regreso a Schuaima*, Ediciones Dauro, Granada-España 2001; *Memorias de Alexander de Brucco*, Editorial Universidad de Antioquia-2002; *Summa poética*, Altazor Editores, 2005; *Camino a Rogitama*, Trilce Editores, 2010; *La Ciudad de las Piedras que cantan*, Caza de libro editores, 2011, y *Temps era Temps*, Gente Nueva Editores, 2013; and *La douce Aniquirone et D`autres poemes somme poètique* (French translation by Marcel Kemadjou Njanke), Gente Nueva Editores, 2014. The novel *Dios puso una sonrisa sobre su rostro*, and the book of essays *Poéticas del Ocultismo en las escrituras de José Antonio Ramos Sucre, Carlos Obregón, César Dávila Andrade y Jaime Sáenz*. He is currently a full time professor at Universidad de Cartagena, Bolívar, Colombia.

Winston Morales Chavarro Neiva-Huila (Colombia), 1969. Comunicador Social y Periodista. Magíster en Estudios de la Cultura, mención Literatura Hispanoamericana, Universidad Andina Simón Bolívar, Quito. Ha recibido numerosos premios literarios entre los que se destaca el Concurso Nacional de Poesía Universidad de Antioquia (2001). Poemas suyos han sido traducidos al inglés, francés, portugués e italiano. Ha publicado los libros de poemas *Aniquirona-* Trilce Editores 1998; *La Lluvia y el ángel* (Coautoría)-Trilce Editores 1999; *De Regreso a Schuaima*, Ediciones Dauro, Granada-España 2001; *Memorias de Alexander de Brucco*, Editorial Universidad de Antioquia-2002; *Summa poética*, Altazor Editores, 2005; *Camino a Rogitama*, Trilce Editores, 2010; *La Ciudad de las Piedras que cantan*, Caza de libro editores, 2011, y *Temps era Temps*, Gente Nueva Editores, 2013; *La douce Aniquirone et D`autres poemes somme poètique* (Traducción al francés de Marcel Kemadjou Njanke), Gente Nueva Editores, 2014; la novela *Dios puso una sonrisa sobre su rostro*, y el libro de ensayo *Poéticas del Ocultismo en las escrituras de José Antonio Ramos Sucre, Carlos Obregón, César Dávila Andrade y Jaime Sáenz.* En la actualidad se desempeña como profesor de tiempo completo en la Universidad de Cartagena, Bolívar, Colombia.

XXVIII
La canción de Lucifer

Mi ídolo de bronce es el abismo
el fuego, las cavernas.

La vida del maldito
-desterrado de la luz y las alturas-
se pendula entre el mal, el bien, lo dionisiaco.

No maldigo de las sombras
no aspiro a las venganzas,
continúo con mi vestidura satánica
instruyéndome en el bien
y solazándome en el mal.

Los más doctos dicen que fui expulsado del espejo,
que mi imagen vagabundea por los laberintos y paradigmas de la muerte.
Pocos saben que conservo mi posición de ángel
que aparezco majestuoso cuando miro mi belleza ante las nubes

que mi sabiduría multiplica la ignominia de los justos
y la nobleza de los desterrados
contagia de belleza a los malditos.

Voy del ascenso al descenso
como el viento que hila los caminos:
no creo en la maldad, en el bien,
en el pasado, en el futuro
pues los cuatro están confinados en las sombras
y las sombras
en el hades de un espejo orbicular.

No maldigo a las alturas
no me duele la caída
hay un punto en que todo deja de ser contradictorio
y nada en este punto se excluye sino que interacciona.

¿Quién ha dicho que el abismo no es la altura?
qué la maldad,- producto de la belleza-,

no es el bien?
que las sombras no son la luz?
que el caído no es el levantado?

Pocos saben que sobrevuelo el infinito,
el paraíso, la manzana,
que mi vestidura de Vampiro
me da el elixir de la noche,
que sustraigo del día los frutos del iluminado
y que espero sabiamente el último camino
para empezar mis andananzas
por la otredad, por la vaguedad,
por lo inmensurable,
por lo indefinible.

EDUARDO LANTIGUA
[R. DOMINICANA]

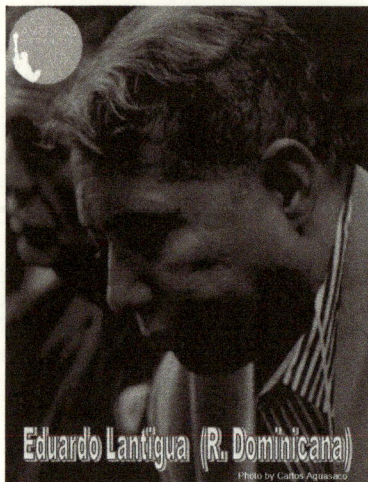

Eduardo Lantigua (R. Dominicana)
Photo by Carlos Aguasaco

Eduardo Lantigua was born in Villa Altagracia, Dominican Republic. He studied technology in DR and Computer Science in Mexico. In literature he is self-taught. His writing has been known in the USA for more than two decades. He has published *Un pez atrapado en el desierto* (Mediabyte 2007), *Ya no estaban las palomas* (MediaIsla 2013) and *La inagotable lectura* (MediaIsla 2013). Some of his critical essays, poems and stories have been included in reputable publications.

Eduardo Lantigua nació en Villa Altagracia, República Dominicana. Estudió Tecnología en RD y Ciencia Computacional en México. En literatura es autodidacta. Su actividad literaria es conocida en los Estados Unidos desde hace ya más de dos décadas. Ha publicado *Un pez atrapado en el desierto* (Mediabyte 2007), *Ya no estaban las palomas* (MediaIsla 2013) Y *La inagotable lectura* (MediaIsla 2013). Ensayos críticos, poemas y relatos suyos han aparecido en importantes publicaciones.

ELEGÍA

A ti, madre.
NO HAY FLORES en tu mirada
solo tu carne y jarrones sin agua
muebles pudriéndose entre las paredes
signo frío sobre dos sillas, las manos vacías,
o memoria de ti equilibrando lo finito
(Terrible contacto de bestia que aletea,
que vigila mis huesos y certifica)
¿Desacierto del silencio?
¿Triunfo de pájaros ensangrentados
que limpian sus picos ardientes
y levantan con estilo sus garras?
No hay flores en tu mirada
solo tu carne y jarrones sin agua
muebles pudriéndose en medio de la sala
¿Quién madre mía,
como Blanca flor de agua te bebe
mariposa como de luz Blanca
te apaga?

Jacqueline Herranz Brooks
[Cuba]

Jacqueline Herranz Brooks (Havana, Cuba, 1968) is a poet, storyteller, visual artist and Spanish instructor. She has published the poetry collection *Liquid Days* (TribalSong, Argentina, 1997), the short stories collection *Escenas para Turistas* (Editorial Campana, NYC, 2003) and the novel *Mujeres sin Trama* (editorial Campana, NYC, 2011). Her writing has been included in anthologies in Spain, Venezuela, Cuba and the USA. In her most recent exhibit, entitled *Maldita Pared: Fotografía y Texto. Cuba / New York*, at Miller Gallery (Jamaica Center for the Arts and Learning), confronting text and images Jacqueline explores the fictionalization of memory. She teaches Spanish at York College and BMCC (CUNY). She is also pursuing doctoral studies in Hispanic and Luso-Brazilian Literatures and Languages at the Graduate Center (CUNY). In her most recent project (Poetry on the street) she pastes texts onto walls around NYC and publishes (electronically) images showing the spaces where they have been displayed.

Jacqueline Herranz Brooks (La Habana, Cuba, 1968) es poeta, narradora, artista visual e instructora de español. Ha publicado el poemario *Liquid Days* (TribalSong, Argentina, 1997), la colección de relatos *Escenas para Turistas* (Editorial Campana, NYC, 2003) y la novela *Mujeres sin Trama* (editorial Campana, NYC, 2011). Sus textos han sido publicados también en diversas antologías en España, Venezuela, Cuba y Estados Unidos. En su más reciente exposición personal interactiva titulada *Maldita Pared: Fotografía y Texto. Cuba / New York*, en la galería Miller de JCAL (Jamaica Center for the Arts and Learning), Jacqueline explora los procesos de ficcionalización de la memoria confrontando imagen y texto. Jacqueline enseña español en York College y BMCC (CUNY) y está estudiando el doctorado en el programa Hispanic and Luso-Brazilian Literaures and Languages en el Graduate Center de NY. Su más reciente proyecto (Poesía en la calle) consiste en pegar textos en las calles de Nueva York y publicar, de manera virtual, las imágenes que muestran los espacios donde estos textos han sido ubicados.

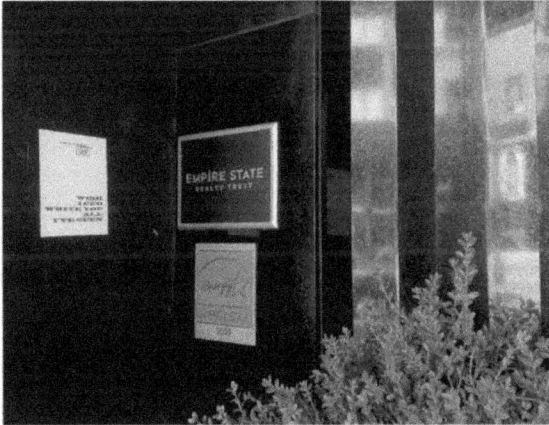

UP TO ~~DAY~~
DATE

WISH
I CUD
WRITE YOU
ALL
I'VE SEEN

JIMMY VALDEZ OSAKU
[R. DOMINICANA]

Jimmy Valdez Osaku (R. Dominicana)
Photo: Keysi Montás

Jimmy Valdez Osaku (6 de Julio 1975) is a poet, painter and cultural activist of Antillean origin. His paintings and art installations have been exhibited in about twenty shows and cultural activities in New York, San Juan, La Habana, Santo Domingo and Madrid. He has coordinated the artistic and cultural events "Dominico-puertorriqueña" and "Uniendo Pueblos". He was the curator and organizer of the art exhibits "Poetas que pintan" 2004, "Undertow" 2012, "6to piso" 2013 and "Te Deum" 2014. Some of his books are *Días enteros para una sopa, Osaku, La redonda peña despeñada, Islamabad queda al norte, Casi tantas lluvias como pájaros, Maruja, Sur Mon Cou etc.* He received the Letras de Ultramar Award in 2009. He lives in NY.

Jimmy Valdez Osaku (6 de Julio 1975) Poeta, pintor, gestor cultural de origen antillano. Sus trabajos pictóricos e instalaciones han sido presentados en una veintena de shows y actividades en New York, San Juan, La Habana, Santo Domingo y Madrid. Ha coordinado las ferias de arte y cultura "Dominico-puertorriqueña" y "Uniendo Pueblos". Organizador y Curador de las exposiciones pictóricas "Poetas que pintan" 2004 "Undertow" 2012, "6to piso" 2013 y "Te Deum" 2014. Algunos de sus libros son: *Días enteros para una sopa, Osaku, La redonda peña despeñada, Islamabad queda al norte, Casi tantas lluvias como pájaros, Maruja, Sur Mon Cou etc.* Premio Letras de Ultramar de literatura 2009. Reside en NY.

X

¿Cómo desayunar esta raíz metida en el asfalto?
¿De qué está hecho lo roto de la infancia, el cuerpo des-
gonzado de una cría, el anidado proyectil en el arco excelso
de las rosas? En cuál de los infinitos habita la desolación,
qué vestigio de piedra pregona en el alma sus escombros,
la herrería filosa de la ballesta? ¿Qué gozo, qué herrumbre,
cuál vocablo de numerosas alas se hunde con lo aberran-
te de las uñas hasta tornar universal lo despiadado? ¿Cómo
dormir, cómo desayunar esta raíz metida en el asfalto, el
odio esparcido en la sutileza de un terrón de azúcar? ¿De
dónde viene la lluvia acida, esta intemperie, el edén des-
memoriado que ha mandado sus fieras contra el mundo?
Busco. Pregunto a los tanques, hablo con los sepultureros;
me invitan a reconocer cualquier trozo de carne. Se queda
en mis ojos la siniestra envoltura tan presta a devorarnos...

MYRNA NIEVES
[PUERTO RICO]

Myrna Nieves is a writer, cultural activist and educator; born in Puerto Rico. A founding member and full professor at Boricua College, she was the director for twenty years of its Winter Poetry Series. Published books are: *Libreta de sueños (narraciones)* (EDUPR, 1997) and *Viaje a la lluvia, poemas* (Mairena, 2003),*Breaking Ground: Anthology of Puerto Rican Women Writers in New York 1980-2012/ Abriendo caminos: antología de escritoras puertorriqueñas en Nueva York* (Campana, 2012), and *El Caribe: paraíso y paradoja. Visiones del intelectual en Alejo Carpentier y Emilio Díaz Valcárcel* (Instituto de Cultura Puertorriqueña, 2012). She is co-author/ co-editor of the collection of poetry and prose *Tripartita: Earth, Dreams, Powers* (Moria, 1990) and the literary publications *Lugar sin límite* (1978), *Guaíza* (1986) and *Moradalsur* (2000). Myrna edited the section of Puerto Rican writers for the anthologies *Mujeres como islas* (fiction, 2002) and *Mujeres como islas II. Poesía* (2011). Awards and recognitions include a Literary Award of the PEN Club of Puerto Rico (1998), Outstanding Latina of the United States by El Diario La Prensa (1998) Award for Extraordinary Contribution to Literature from the National Federation of Puerto Rican Pioneers (2001) and the Poetry and Education Award from the Instituto de Puerto Rico (NY, 2013).

Myrna Nieves es una escritora y educadora nacida en Puerto Rico. Es miembro fundador y catedrática de Boricua College, donde dirigió por 20 años la Serie Invernal de Poesía, que presentó numerosos escritores puertorriqueños, caribeños y latinoamericanos en Nueva York. Ha publicado

Libreta de sueños (narraciones) (EDUPR, 1997, Premio de Cuento del PEN Club de Puerto Rico 1998), *Viaje a la lluvia, poemas* (Mairena, 2003), *El Caribe: paraíso y paradoja. Visiones del intelectual en Alejo Carpentier y Emilio Díaz Valcárcel* y *Breaking Ground: Anthology of Puerto Rican Women Writers in New York 1980-2012/ Abriendo caminos: antología de escritoras puertorriqueñas en Nueva York 1980-2012* (2012). Es co-autora y co-editora de *Tripartita: Earth, Dreams, Powers* (1990), *Lugar sin límite* (1978), *Guaíza* (1986) y *Moradalsur* (2000). Es, además, co-autora y compiladora de la sección de Puerto Rico en la antologías *Mujeres como islas* (narrativa, 2002) y *Mujeres como islas II. Poesía* (2011). Reconocimientos: Premio de Cuento del PEN Club de Puerto Rico (1998), Premio Latinas Destacadas de Estados Unidos de El Diario La Prensa de Nueva York (1998), Premio "Contribución Extraordinaria a la Literatura" de la Federación Nacional de Pioneros Puertorriqueños (2001) y Premio de Educación y Poesía del Instituto de Puerto Rico (2013).

PIGEON

I already know that you like campuses and cafés
And I remember you like that…
I remember you speaking of those days
of glory and silhouettes
With eyes that know of colors and distances
Marginal in your dreams of an adult child
As you walk through rooftops
Strong wind blowing

But as for me
I like the plazas of small towns
Or the silent parks filled with rain
I like to stand facing the river
As a rusty ship forming in the fog
Blares out the lives of people I don't know

And then
Imagining myself
I would like to be another person in a strange land
I would like to speak many languages, be unique
I would like to be nameless
I would like to be a dove

Translated from the Spanish by Zaadia Colón

PALOMA

Ya sé que te gustan los campus y los cafés
y te recuerdo así
comentando los días de gloria y las siluetas
con esos ojos que saben de colores y de distancias
marginal en tus sueños de niño grande
cuando caminas por las azoteas llenas de viento

Pero a mí
pensándolo bien
me gustan las plazas de los pueblos chicos
o los parques silenciosos llenos de lluvia
me gusta pararme frente al río
e imaginarme un barco mohoso en la neblina
que bocina vidas de gentes que no conozco

Y entonces
adivinándola
quisiera ser otra persona en un país extraño
quisiera hablar muchas lenguas, quisiera ser distinta
quisiera no tener nombre
quisiera ser paloma

KEISELIM A. MONTÁS
[R. DOMINICANA]

Keiselim A. Montás (Keysi) was born in the Dominican Republic in 1968; in 1985 immigrated to the US (Queens, New York), where he finished high school, got a BA in Spanish and Secondary Education from Queens College and then an MA in Spanish Literature from the University of Cincinnati. In addition to publishing poems, photos, short stories, essays and literary interviews in various magazines from *Queens College, Columbia University*, and *The University of New Mexico*, he has published: *Poemas Diurnos*, (poems, plaquette, New York,1992 y 2005); *Amor de ciudad grande* (poems, New York, 2006); *Reminiscencias* (Letras de Ultramar 2006, Prize Winner, short stories, Santo Domingo, 2007); *Allá (diario del transtierro)* (poems, New York-New Hampshire, 2012 and digital version 2013); "Historia de mudos" (short story) appears in *Viajeros del rocío* (anthology containing 25 Dominican fiction writers who write from abroad), Santo Domingo, 2008; "Martín, el mejor cuento del mundo" (short story) and various poems appear in *Nostalgias de Arena* (anthology of writers from Dominican communities in the US), Santo Domingo, 2011. His short story "Sin lágrimas" won First Prize in the XIX Concurso de Cuentos Radio Santa María 2012, La Vega, República Dominicana. Most recently, 5 of his micro-short stories appear in the anthology *Shortstop microrrelatos de béisbol dominicano*, Letra Negra, Ediciones Ferilibro (Guatemala, 2014). Currently, he lives in New Hampshire and works at Dartmouth College, where in addition to his regular functions as Associate Director of Safety and Security has also served as *Faculty Fellow* for the Tucker Foundation Alternative Spring Break Trip to the Dominican Republic. He has worked in the Public Safety industry for over 25 years, mainly within higher education.

Keiselim A. Montás: Santo Domingo, República Dominicana, 1968. Desde 1985 vive en EE.UU., donde terminó sus estudios secundarios e hizo una licenciatura y una maestría en lengua y literatura castellanas. Además de publicar poemas sueltos, fotos, cuentos, ensayos y entrevistas literarias en revistas de *Queens College, Columbia University,* y *The University of New Mexico* ha publicado: *Pequeños Poemas Diurnos,* (poemas, plaquette, New York,1992 y 2005); *Amor de ciudad grande* (poemas, New York, 2006); *Reminiscencias* (Premio Letras de Ultramar 2006, cuentos, Santo Domingo, 2007); *Allá (diario del transtierro)* (poemas, New York-New Hampshire, 2012 y versión digital 2013); "Historia de mudos" (cuento) aparece en *Viajeros del rocío* (antología que registra a 25 narradores dominicanos que escriben desde el extranjero), Santo Domingo, 2008; "Martín, el mejor cuento del mundo" (cuento) y varios de sus poemas aparecen en *Nostalgias de Arena* (antología de escritores de las comunidades dominicanas en los Estados Unidos), Santo Domingo, 2011. Su cuento "Sin lágrimas" fue ganador del primer lugar en el XIX Concurso de Cuentos Radio Santa María 2012, La Vega, República Dominicana. Más recientemente, 5 de sus microrrelatos aparecen en la antología *Shortstop microrrelatos de béisbol dominicano,* Letra Negra, Ediciones Ferilibro (Guatemala, 2014). En la actualidad vive en New Hampshire y trabaja en Dartmouth College donde ha desempeña la función de *Faculty Fellow,* además de su cargo permanente como Director Asociado del Departamento de Seguridad. Ha trabajado en el sector de la seguridad pública por más de 25 años, principalmente en el área de educación universitaria.

We are going about, my brother and I, with needle and thread (no thimble)
asting the contours of a broken cloth:
How does one mend that which has been broken for so long;
that which has never been whole?
We are a sheet of remnants, of all sorts,
that we have been sewing together as our blanket and our shield;
piece by piece, remnant by remnant
thread and needle (no thimble)
stitch by stitch.
Today we have a huge calico which covers and protects us from the cold and
the heat;
nonetheless,
our fingers are aching and torn from sewing so much without thimble,
from so much sewing without having anyone to sew for us.
And today, after almost 5 earned degrees,
a domestic and an industrial sewing machine,
we continue to baste with needle and thread (no thimble)
the broken seams on the skin our fingertips,
mending ourselves although it does not stop hurting.

08:09 a.m.
June 8, 2002
New York, New York

Andamos mi hermano y yo con hilo y aguja (sin dedal)
hilvanándonos los contornos de un lienzo roto:
¿cómo remendar lo que hace tanto que está roto;
lo que nunca estuvo completo?
Somos una sábana de retazos, de toda clase,
que hemos ido cosiendo como nuestra cobija y nuestro escudo;
pedazo a pedazo, retazo a retazo
hilo y aguja (sin dedal)
puntada a puntada.
Hoy tenemos una gran manta que nos cubre y nos protege del frío y del
calor;
sin embargo,
tenemos los dedos dolidos y destrozados de tanto coser sin dedal,
de tanto coser sin que nadie cosa por nosotros.
Y hoy, después de casi 5 títulos universitarios,
una máquina de coser casera y otra industrial,
seguimos hilvanando con hilo y aguja (sin dedal)
las costuras rotas en la piel de las yemas de los dedos:
nos remendamos aunque no deje de doler.

08:09 a.m.
8 de junio, 2002
New York, New York

KARINA RIEKE
[R. DOMINICANA]

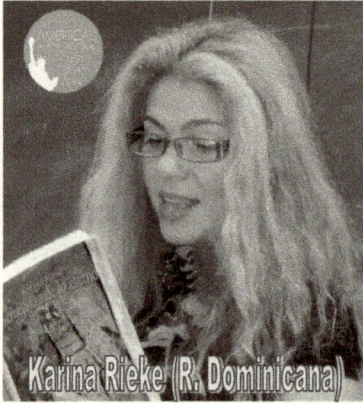

Karina Rieke was born in the Domincan Republic. She studied photography, painting and ceramics at the City College of New York. She also attended the MA program in Creative Writing at CCNY. Currently, she is completing graduate studies in Mental Health Counseling at Manhattan College. She has published: *Semejanza de lo Eterno* (2002), *Mitología* del Instante (2009) and *Ontología de la palabra* (2013). Her work has been included in several anthologies.

Karina Rieke nació en la República Dominicana. Estudió fotografía, pintura y cerámica en City College of New York. También adelantó estudios de maestría en escritura creativa en la misma universidad. En la actualidad adelanta estudios de postgrado en consejería en salud mental en Manhattan College. Ha publicado los libros *Semejanza de lo Eterno* (2002), *Mitología* del Instante (2009) y *Ontología de la palabra* (2013). Su trabajo ha sido incluido en varias antologías.

DE FRENTE A MI ESTATURA

Mujer repite tu silencio
Y estira con palabras tu dolor
Tú de sonrisa angular
Cruces de razones te atormentan mientras
El enorme cielo impone tu misterio

Acariciándote desconocida
Descubro
Tus otras estaciones

Mujer repite tu silencio
Y celebra desatando tus temores

Tú de vanidad estirada cargando
Cementerio de razones
Vaticinas en voz tus agonías
Sentenciando la ternura que intimida

Mujer repite tu silencio
Para conciliarme antiguamente
En tus palabras
Irremisiblemente luminosas
De agonías

Dame tu espalda
Para negarte y negarme
Códigos que me incorporan
Vigilan tus verdades

Galería de dioses ajenos
Niegan el oficio de tu voz
Hoy mías
Y solo rechazando tu alma
Alimento mi sentencia

Mujer que sujetando tu nombre
Soy tu gozo

Déjame acariciar tus bestias
Que esparces al sonido
Como muelle de avenencias

Tú de carnes vírgenes
Falso festín de palabras pálidas que
Avejentas mis miradas

Mujer repite tu silencio
Y déjame reemplazar
Tus inciviles
Espaciosas manos
Contenidas
Desesperadas
De frente a mi estatura

Ven y dame tu silencio
Que en otro sitio será
Que te descubro

CAROLINA ZAMUDIO
[ARGENTINA]

Carolina Zamudio (1973) was born in Curuzú Cuatiá, Corrientes, Argentina. She studied journalism at Universidad Católica Argentina. Thanks to a scholarship, she earned a Master's degree in communications and public affairs. She received the 'Universitarios Siglo XXI' award by Diario La Nación. She works in journalism and communications and conducted the radio series "Los libros no muerden". Since 2007 she has resided in Abu Dhabi, Ginebra and Barranquilla. Her poetry collection *Seguir al viento* was recently launched at the mythic literary cafe La Cueva in Barranquilla and also in Argentina. She has an unpublished poetry collection entitled *La oscuridad de lo que brilla*.

Carolina Zamudio nació en 1973 en Curuzú Cuatiá, Corrientes, Argentina. Periodista por la Universidad Católica Argentina. Obtuvo mediante una beca una Maestría en Comunicación Institucional y Asuntos Públicos. Ganó el Premio 'Universitarios Siglo XXI' del Diario La Nación. Trabaja en Periodismo y Comunicaciones. Condujo el ciclo radial "Los libros no muerden". Desde 2007 ha resido en: Abu Dhabi (Emiratos Árabes Unidos), Ginebra (Suiza) y Barranquilla (Colombia). *Seguir al viento*, poemario, fue recientemente presentado en Colombia -La Cueva, mítico recinto literario en Barranquilla- y también en la Argentina, en Buenos Aires y su ciudad natal. Tiene inédito el libro *La oscuridad de lo que brilla*.

CENTER AND END

I

The last embrace
before the first death
a frank flirting with madness
the time we made love
and it was a well
as absolute as the cosmos
the original breath from some diffuse beyond
of the only truth:
birth.

II

Life isn't there
not even then.
This is life
this breath, this skin
the sensation of a dry well
an abandoned hive
the center and the end.

III

Emptiness has the weight
of the absolute
never less. Center.
Emptiness is
the measure of the world.

CENTRO Y FIN

I

El último abrazo
antes de la primera muerte
el franco coqueteo con la locura
la vez que hicimos el amor
y fue un pozo
absoluto como el cosmos
el aliento originario de un más allá difuso
de la única verdad
que es el nacimiento.

II

La vida no está allá
ni entonces.
La vida es ésta
este aliento, esta piel
esta sensación de pozo seco
de colmena abandonada
de centro y de fin.

III

El vacío tiene el peso
de lo absoluto
nunca menos. Centro.
Lo vacío es
la medida del mundo.

Kianny N. Antigua
[R. Dominicana]

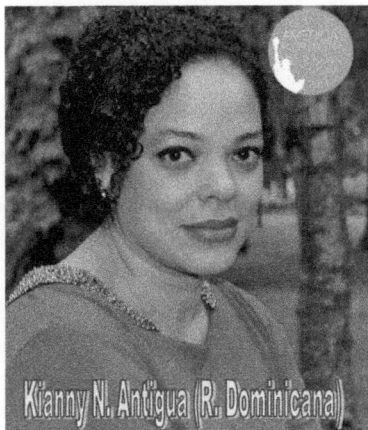

Kianny N. Antigua (Dominican Republic). She has published *Mía, Esteban y las nuevas palabras / Mía, Esteban and the New Words* (cuento infantil, Alfaguara 2014), *El tragaluz del sótano* (cuento, Artepoética Press 2014), *Cuando el resto se apaga* (poesía, Proyecto Zompopos 2013), *9 Iris y otros malditos cuentos* (Editora Nacional 2010) and *El expreso* (cuento, Argos 2004). Some of her stories have been translated to Italian, French and English. Her work also appears in several anthologies, textbooks, magazines and other media outlets.

Kianny N. Antigua (República Dominicana) Ha publicado: *Mía, Esteban y las nuevas palabras / Mía, Esteban and the New Words* (cuento infantil, Alfaguara 2014), *El tragaluz del sótano* (cuento, Artepoética Press 2014), *Cuando el resto se apaga* (poesía, Proyecto Zompopos 2013), *9 Iris y otros malditos cuentos* (Editora Nacional 2010) y *El expreso* (cuento, Argos 2004). Algunos de sus relatos además han sido traducidos al italiano, al francés y al inglés. Además, sus trabajos literarios aparecen en múltiples antologías, libros de textos, revistas y otros medios.

IT IS NO LONGER ABOUT FRUITS NOR THE SOUTH

Strange pieces fall from the sky.
The trees' humpback
could not take the weight
nor the sadness.

The explosion of a gigantic fruit
floods the air upon falling,
and its pulp scatters about
staining sidewalks and memory.

The road simply has rotten man.
Strange times,
strange God.

YA NO ES COSA DE FRUTAS NI DE SOUTH

Extraños pedazos caen del cielo.
La joroba de los árboles
no pudo con el peso
ni con la tristeza.

El estallido de una fruta gigantesca,
al caer, inunda el viento
y la pulpa se esparce
manchando las aceras y la memoria.

El camino sólo ha podrido al hombre.
Extraños los tiempos,
extraño Dios.

CHRISTIAN CUARTAS
[COLOMBIA]

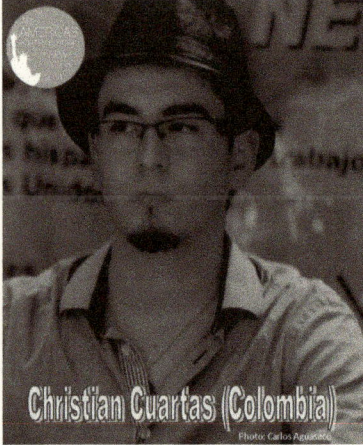

Christian Cuartas (Colombia)
Photo: Carlos Aguasaco

Christian Cuartas was born in Cali, Colombia. He has resided in New York since 2008. He is a poet, political and cultural activist, independent interpreter and attends The City University of New York (CUNY). He is a member of 'Poetas en Nueva York'. His work has been published in the newspaper *Vecindad* that he helps to coordinate.

Christian Cuartas nació en Cali, Colombia. Reside en Nueva York desde el 2008. Poeta, activista político y cultural, intérprete independiente y estudiante de CUNY. Miembro del Colectivo 'Poetas en Nueva York'. Ha sido publicado en el periódico cultural *Vecindad*, donde participa en el comité organizador.

ERES ARENA EN ZAPATO

Eres arena en zapato.
Caballo sin herradura.
Un libro sin última página.

Zapato en arena eres.
Herradura sin caballo.
Una última página sin libro.

Una huella de herradura en la arena,
un caballo sin zapatos despide la última página.

María Farazdel
[R. Dominicana]

Maria Farazdel is a native of the Dom. Republic who has lived and worked in NY since the age of 17. She received her B.A. from Hunter College, M.A. in education from Fordham University and P.D. in School District Administration from Long Island University; Formally an Assistant Principal. She has taught English as a Second Language and Bilingual Education. She is a member of 'Dominican Poets USA" and the literary group Camila Enriquez Ureña. Some of her work appears in the anthologies: "From a Window" in the US. *New poetry and narrative Hispano American in Spain* and *Poetas de la Era I, II* in Dom. Republic. She is the author of the books: *My Little Paradise, Amongst Voice and Spaces* and *Laberinto de la Espera*.

María Farazdel nació en Rep. Dom. Emigro a NYC a los 17 años donde recibió una licenciatura de Hunter College en Arte y francés, una maestría en pedagogía e inglés como Segundo Idioma en la Universidad de Fordham. Adquirió un P.D. en administración escolar en la Universidad de Long Island (CWP). Ejerció como subdirectora en una escuela de Nueva York. Ha sido profesora de inglés como segundo idioma y educación bilingüe. Forma parte de los poetas dominicanos en USA y del grupo literario 'Camila Enríquez Ureña'. Figura en las antologías: *From a Window en los Estados Unidos, nueva poesía y narrativa hispanoamericana en España* y *Poetas de la Era I, II* en la Republica Dominicana. Autora de los libros *My Little Paradise, Entre Voces y Espacios* y *Laberinto de la Espera* (inédito).

FOOTPRINTS

Like the wind stirring up what has been lost. . .

I return to look for them to no avail:
dismembered, they left with the echo of the world

Misplaced, abandoned, bewitched
to the beat of "New York, New York"

Scattered leaves, pigeon droppings
they let their owner loose to raindrops

Meanwhile,
the ocean drinks up my groove,
my recollections,
splashing the shifting of memory:
"Blowing in the wind" Bob Dylan
is singing.

HUELLAS

Estas huellas
como el viento agitan lo perdido…
persiguen mi sombra

En vano regreso a buscarlas:
desmembradas se fueron con el eco del mundo
al ritmo de New York, New York

Hojas derramadas, boñigas de pichón /
desatan su dueño a gotas

Mientras
el Hudson se bebe mi surco, mi recuerdo,
salpicando el tránsito de la memoria:
"Blowing in the Wind," tararea Bob Dylan.

OSIRIS MOSQUEA
[R. DOMINICANA]

Osiris Mosquea was born in San Francisco de Macorís, Dominican Republic. She attended Universidad Autónoma de Santo Domingo (U.A.S.D.) where she earned a BA in accounting. She is a cultural activist, founder and coeditor of *Revista Trazos*. Her work has been included in anthologies, magazines and newspapers in several countries. She has published the poetry collections *Raga del Tiempo*, 2009 and *Viandante en Nueva York*, 2013.

Osiris Mosquea nació en San Francisco de Macorís, República Dominicana. Realizó sus estudios universitarios en la Universidad Autónoma de Santo Domingo (U.A.S.D.) donde obtuvo su título de Licenciada en Contabilidad. Es gestora cultural, fundadora y coeditora de la revista *Trazos*. Sus escritos han sido publicados en revistas, antologías, y periódicos de varios países. Tiene publicado dos libros de poesía: *Raga del Tiempo*, 2009 y *Viandante en Nueva York*, 2013.

THE CITY

The worst is not the sorrow or the lie
But having lost the route back to Paradise.
Pedro Antonio Valdez

The city lays dressed with shadows
Seven square miles of watercolors
Paint a drunken smile on any corner

Men without destiny
From five to ten counting the efforts
Lost in memories and evocations
Marked in their faces
Murdered by boredom
Continue in the womb
Who deceives them

The night
Multiplied
Blurred in spades of light
Is always awaken

The city
Hides in its sewage
Subways and neon lights
The American dream
Accomplice of the savage code and the sophism

While there continue to be one thousand reasons
In any corner
To slice your wrists with a needle
Inhale some dust to alleviate the senses
And kill in some way or another
These new prank of our destiny.

Kill
Kill

Kill the reason sitting on the sidewalks
And then what does another drink will do
To cheat the dreams with the Hudson…

LA CIUDAD

> *Lo peor no es la mentira ni la pena*
> *sino el haber extraviado la vuelta al paraíso.*
> Pedro Antonio Valdez

La ciudad
yace vestida de sombras
siete Kilómetros de acuarelas
pintan una sonrisa borracha
en las esquinas.

Hombres sin destino
de cinco a diez contados los sudores
perdidos en evocaciones y memorias
marcados sus rostros
asesinados por el tedio
permanecen vástago del vientre lascivo
que lo engaña.

La noche
multiplicada
difuminada en espadas de luces
permanece despierta.

La ciudad esconde en las cloacas
subterráneos y neones
el American-dream
cómplice del código salvaje
y del sofisma.

Mientras
siguen en las esquinas
las mil razones para cortarse las venas
inhalar el polvo que aniquila los sentidos
matar de alguna forma
esta maldita cabriola del destino.

Matar
matar
matar la razón
sentada en las calzadas
y entonces
de que sirve un trago más
para engañar los sueños sobre el Hudson?

ROLANDO PÉREZ
[CUBA]

Rolando Pérez (Cuba) is a professor of Hispanic American Literature in Hunter College (CUNY). He received a BA in philosophy from the College of New Jersey and two masters in philosophy and literature from Stony Brook (SUNY). He earned a Ph.D. in Spanish and Hispanic American Literature at The Graduate Center of CUNY. Among his books and articles are: *Severo Sarduy and the Religion of the Text* (UP of America, 1988*); On An(archy) and Schizoanalysis* (Autonomedia/Semiotext(e), 1990); "Vallejo on Language and Politics", *Letras hispanas: Revista de literatura y cultura* 5 (2008); "Irony, Love, and Political Economy in José Asunción Silva's *De sobremesa*", *Hispanófila* 150 (2007); "The Sadean Poetics of Solitude in Paz and Pizarnik",*Latin American Literary Review* 33 (2005); "The Proto Liberation Theology of César Vallejo and the Philosophy of Emmanuel Levinas and Enrique Dussel", *Double Edges*. Ed. William Watkins. New York: SUNY Press (2012); y "El barroco de Severo Sarduy: hacia una ética transatlántica", *Galerna: revista internacional de literatura* (2012). He is also the author of several fiction books, plays and poetry collections including *The Lining of Our Souls: Excursions into selected paintings of Edward Hopper (Cool Grove Press 2002); The Electric Comedy* (Cool Grove 2000); and *The Divine Duty of Servants* (Based on drawings by Bruno Schulz; Cool Grove 1999). Some of his work was included in *The Norton Anthology of Latino Literature* (2011). His most recent book is *Severo Sarduy and the Neo-Baroque Image of Thought in the Visual Arts* (Purdue UP, 2011).

Rolando Pérez (Cuba) es profesor de literatura hispanoamericana en el Departamento de Romance Languages de Hunter College (CUNY). Es licenciado en Filosofía por el College of New Jersey, con dos Maestrías, una en Filosofía y otra en Literatura hispánica por la Universidad de Stony Brook (SUNY), y un Doctorado en Literatura española e hispanoamericana por el Graduate Center de la City University of New York. Entre sus libros y artículos cabe destacar: *Severo Sarduy and the Religion of the Text* (UP of America, 1988*); On An(archy) and Schizoanalysis* (Autonomedia/Semiotext(e), 1990); "Vallejo on Language and Politics", *Letras hispanas: Revista de literatura y cultura* 5 (2008); "Irony, Love, and Political Economy in José Asunción Silva's *De sobremesa*", *Hispanófila* 150 (2007); "The Sadean Poetics of Solitude in Paz and Pizarnik",*Latin American Literary Review* 33 (2005); "The Proto Liberation Theology of César Vallejo and the Philosophy of Emmanuel Levinas and Enrique Dussel", *Double Edges.* Ed. William Watkins. New York: SUNY Press (2012); y "El barroco de Severo Sarduy: hacia una ética transatlántica", *Galerna: revista internacional de literatura* (2012). Rolando Pérez es también autor de varios libros de ficción, obras de teatro, y poesía en prosa, entre ellos, *The Lining of Our Souls: Excursions into selected paintings of Edward Hopper (Cool Grove Press 2002); The Electric Comedy* (una versión postmoderna de la *Divina Comedia*; Cool Grove 2000); y *The Divine Duty of Servants* (prosa basada en los dibujos de Bruno Schulz; Cool Grove 1999). Selecciones de algunas de sus obras literarias aparecen en la antología, *The Norton Anthology of Latino Literature* (2011). Su más reciente publicación se titula *Severo Sarduy and the Neo-Baroque Image of Thought in the Visual Arts* (Purdue UP, 2011).

CANTO 1 [36]

In the beginning was the flesh,
and the flesh became word,
and the word became memory,
and our memory became electric.
Then in a puff of smoke,
gone was the age of the Ancestors,
gone was the age of History.
The exteriors all changed.

The desert, the artic,
And everything in between disappeared-
or more accurately, reappeared as something other.
Something few of us had ever seen;
a brave new world,
born of a bloodless womb.
Some of us –the brave ones– got
on our vehicles and set out
to explore the new world:
hoping to find the promised signs of a new life.
But when we got there,
there was nothing.
A deception, a lie:
the interior had not changed at all.
Disappointed,
Some of us returned
blinded by artificial stars, and worse,
some of us did not return at all:
trapped in a web,
impossible to escape.
And yet most of the inhabitants
here believe that this is the best
of all possible worlds:
safe, clean, secure, and ethical.
But where is the blood?
Where is the body?
And this thing of an "artificial mind,"
what could this possibly be?
Anyone who has studied philosophy
knows that a virtual substance
is a contradiction in terms.
"Yes, but as everyone here knows,
thanks to electricity
the ARTIFICIAL becomes the REAL,"
I am reminded by an eager young man,
full of potential,
lacking in qualities.
Thus our dreams, our nightmares,
our longings, and our desires
have become electric, subtle,

even transparent.
No more chains,
no more pulleys…
but electric pulses
transferred at excessive speeds
by our "new and improved"
desiring machines.

Translated by Óscar Curieses

CANTO 1 [36]

Al principio fue la carne,
y la carne se hizo palabra,
y la palabra se hizo memoria,
y nuestra memoria se hizo eléctrica.
Luego en un soplo de humo,
desapareció la edad de los Ancestros,
desapareció la edad de la Historia.
Todos los exteriores cambiaron.
El desierto, el ártico,
y todo lo que se encontraba entre ellos se desvaneció,
o con más precisión, reapareció como otra cosa.
Muy pocos de nosotros lo vimos;
un mundo feliz
nacido de un útero sin sangre.
Algunos de nosotros -los valientes- montamos
en nuestros vehículos y salimos
a explorar el nuevo mundo:
esperando encontrar los signos prometidos de una
nueva vida.
Pero cuando llegamos allí,
no había nada.
Un engaño, una mentira:
el interior no había cambiado en absoluto.
Decepcionados,

algunos de nosotros regresamos
cegados por estrellas artificiales, y lo que es peor
algunos de nosotros nunca regresamos:
atrapados en una red
de la que era imposible escapar.
Con todo, aquí muchos de los habitantes,
piensan que este es el mejor
de los mundos posibles:
protegido, limpio, seguro y ético.
Pero, ¿dónde está la sangre?
¿Dónde está el cuerpo?
Y esta cosa llamada "mente artificial",
¿qué puede realmente ser?
Cualquiera que haya estudiado filosofía
sabe que una sustancia virtual
es un contrasentido.
"Sí, pero como todos saben aquí,
gracias a la electricidad
lo ARTIFICIAL se convierte en lo REAL",
me lo recuerda un jovencito insaciable,
lleno de potencial
pero falto de atributos.
Así, nuestros sueños, nuestras pesadillas,
nuestros anhelos, nuestros deseos
se han hecho eléctricos, sutiles,
incluso transparentes.
No más cadenas,
no más poleas…
sino pulsaciones eléctricas
transferidas a una velocidad excesiva
por nuestras "nuevas y mejoradas"
máquinas deseantes.

YVELISSE FANITH
[R. DOMINICANA]

Yvelisse Fanith (R. Dominicana)

Photo: José Oquendo

Yvelisse Fanith was born in the Dominican Republic whe she completed her basic education. In 1967 she moved to New York where she attended the Fashion Institute of Technology. She has published the poetry collections *Orígenes y Tiempos* (2005), *Realidad del sueño* (2011) and *Danza Almagre* (2014). Her poetry has been included in several national and international anthologies.

Yvelisse Fanith nace en República Dominicana donde realiza sus estudios primarios y de escuela superior. En el año 1967 se traslada a New York, Estados Unidos y allí, estudia diseño de modas en el Fashion InstituteofTechnology de New York. Ha publicado los poemarios *Orígenes y Tiempos* (2005), *Realidad del sueño* (2011) y *Danza Almagre* (2014). Sus trabajos poéticos han sido publicados en diversas antologías nacionales e internacionales.

MERIDIANA

Cuando la vida hiere
y te muere la muerte
y el cielo se derrama en fría lluvia
y mil pájaros brotan de una azulada fosa…
No es la hora

Cuando la vida hiere
y te muere la muerte
y cabalgas al dorso de la desesperanza
y un quejido largo…largo
interrumpe el sueño de los vivos…
No es la hora

Cuando la vida hiere
y te muere la muerte
y sientes que el cielo se recoge
en siniestra estocada
lo mismo que a las cinco de la tarde…
Casi es hora

Cuando la vida hiere
y te muere la muerte
y se te nublan de Lorca los sentidos
y retornan los pájaros
sedientos a su fosa
entonces…
Es la hora.

MIGUEL ÁNGEL ZAPATA
[PERÚ]

Miguel Ángel Zapata is a Peruvian poet and essayist. He has published collections of poetry, translations and prose. Among his books are *La ventana y once poemas* (México, 2014), *La lluvia siempre sube* (Buenos Aires, 2012), *Fragmentos de una manzana y otros poemas* (Sevilla, 2011), *Ensayo sobre la rosa. Poesía selecta 1983-2008* (Lima, 2010), *Los canales de piedra. Antología mínima* (Venezuela, 2008), *Un pino me habla de la lluvia* (Lima, 2007), *Iguana* (Lima, 2006), *Los muslos sobre la grama* (Buenos Aires, 2005), *Cuervos* (México, 2003), *El cielo que me escribe* (México, 2002), *Lumbre de la letra* (Lima, 1997), *Escribir bajo el polvo* (Lima, 2000), *Poemas para violín y orquesta* (México, 1991), and *Imágenes los juegos* (Lima, 1987). His poems have been translated to English, French, Italian, Portuguese, Arabic and Russian. He has also published the volumes *Vuela un cuervo sobre la luna. Muestra de poesía española contemporánea: 1959-1980* (Nueva York, 2014). *La voz deudora. Conversaciones sobre poesía hispanoamericana* (Lima- México, 2013), *Vapor trasatlántico. Estudios sobre poesía hispánica y norteamericana* (Lima-Nueva York, 2008), *El hacedor y las palabras. Diálogos con la poesía de América Latina* (Lima-México, 2005), among others. He is a professor of Hispanic Literature at Hofstra University in New York.

Miguel Ángel Zapata, poeta y ensayista peruano, ha publicado libros de poesía, ensayo, traducción y prosa. Entre sus libros de poesía figuran: *La ventana y once poemas* (México, 2014), *La lluvia siempre sube* (Buenos Aires, 2012), *Fragmentos de una manzana y otros poemas* (Sevilla, 2011), *Ensayo sobre la rosa. Poesía selecta 1983-2008* (Lima, 2010), *Los canales de piedra. Antología mínima* (Venezuela, 2008), *Un pino me habla de la lluvia* (Lima, 2007), *Iguana*(Lima, 2006), *Los muslos sobre la grama* (Buenos Aires, 2005), *Cuervos* (México, 2003), *El cielo que me escribe* (México, 2002), *Lumbre de la letra* (Lima, 1997), *Escribir bajo el polvo* (Lima, 2000), *Poemas para violín y orquesta* (México, 1991), e *Imágenes los juegos* (Lima, 1987). Su poesía ha sido traducida al inglés, francés, italiano, portugués, árabe y ruso. Ha publicado también los volúmenes: *Vuela un cuervo sobre la luna. Muestra de poesía española contemporánea: 1959-1980* (Nueva York, 2014). *La voz deudora. Conversaciones sobre poesía hispanoamericana* (Lima- México, 2013), *Vapor trasatlántico. Estudios sobre poesía hispánica y norteamericana* (Lima-Nueva York, 2008), *El hacedor y las palabras. Diálogos con la poesía de América Latina* (Lima- México, 2005), entre otros. Es profesor de Literaturas hispánicas en Hofstra University, Nueva York.

THIGHS UPON THE GRASS

I am writing because of the girl I saw jogging this morning in the cemetery, the one who floated against the dead. She ran and her body was a feather that swayed against death. Then I said in this kingdom sports were good not only for the heart's delight but also for the orgasm of sight. Seeing her run in her little transparent shorts I concluded that cemeteries don't have to be sad, and that the girl's steady gallop gave the landscape another perspective; the sun took on a reddish hue, its vague light giving life to her skin, her golden hair shining upon the gravestones and again I thought that death was not the subject of tears but rather of joy when life continued vibrating upon the grass.

Newly revised version, first published in Suzanne Jill Levine, Reckoning, Finishing Line Press (Georgetown, Kentucky, 2012).

Translation by Suzanne Jill Levine

LOS MUSLOS SOBRE LA GRAMA

Escribo por la muchacha que vi correr esta mañana por el cementerio, la que trotaba ágilmente sobre los muertos. Ella corría y su cuerpo era una pluma de ave que se mecía contra la muerte. Entonces dije que en este reino el deporte no era bueno solo para la alegría del corazón sino también para el orgasmo de la vista. Al verla correr con sus pequeños shorts transparentes deduje que los cementerios no tenían por qué ser tristes, el galope acompasado de la chica daba otra perspectiva al paisaje: el sol adquiría un tono rojizo, su luz tenue se clavaba dando vida a la piel, los mausoleos brillaban con su cabellera de oro, y volví a pensar que la muerte no era un tema de lágrimas sino más bien de gozo cuando la vida continuaba vibrando con los muslos sobre la grama.

ALEXIS ROMAY
[CUBA-USA]

Alexis Romay (Cuba) received a BA in Education and an MA in Hispanic American Literature. He is the author of the novels *La apertura cubana* and *Salidas de emergencia*, the collection of sonnets *Los culpables* and *Diversionismo ideológico*. He has collaborated with magazines such as *Encuentro de la Cultura Cubana*, *Caleta*, *Replicante* and *Letras Libres*. Alexis lives in New Jersey with his wife, his son, his dogs and several books.

Alexis Romay (Cuba) obtuvo una licenciatura en Educación y una maestría en Lengua y Literatura Hispanoamericana. Es autor de las novelas *La apertura cubana* y *Salidas de emergencia*, el libro de sonetos *Los culpables*, así como de *Diversionismo ideológico*. Ha colaborado con las revistas *Encuentro de la Cultura Cubana*, *Caleta*, *Replicante* y *Letras Libres*. Vive en Nueva Jersey, con su esposa, su hijo, sus perros y varios libros.

Homo cubensis (whitman 2.0)

Me cito y me celebro a mí mismo,
y lo que tuiteo de mí debes retuitear,
pues cada carácter mío también te pertenece.
Me congratulo e invito a mis seguidores
a que me incluyan en sus favoritos;
y me inclino y contemplo plácidamente
como crece la hierba en las redes sociales.
Mi lengua, cada átomo de mi sangre,
formado en otro suelo, en otro aire,
nacido allá, de padres que nacieron allá,
cuyas madres y abuelas repitieron la hazaña
irrepetible de nacer, crecer y morir allá,
y ese catauro interminable que el lugar común
ha dado en denominar "mis raíces",
me obligan a redactar este verso en español,
y heme aquí, ahora, a estos años incontables
—con una lista de lectores
que crece y decrece con las mareas
y mi opinión sobre el ser cubano—,
declarándome dispuesto a continuar la parranda.
Los grupos en Facebook, esa otra forma de malvivir,
ese estado de apatía que se acerca a la cosa en sí
para luego evitarla, me invitan
a cultivar Dios sabe qué en alguna granja,
o a intercambiar palabras con amigos,
o a jugar un partido de ajedrez,
o a que les dé mi santo y, ya que estamos, seña,
y se conforman con lo que son, y han olvidado.
Yo conservo la memoria, mal que me pese,
y me permito escribir en todo momento
sobre la naturaleza mía, que es tu naturaleza,
que es la naturaleza de quienes han leído estas líneas
y prometo hacerlo hasta el fin de los días,
cuando me apaguen el Morro de una vez y por siempre.

ANA ISABEL SAILLANT
[R. DOMINICANA]

Ana Isabel Saillant Valerio was born in Santiago de los Caballeros, Dominican Republic. She has resided in New York since 1973, and holds a Master's degree in Bilingual Education. She also earned a BA on Elemental Education from City College of New York. She attended the Universidad Autonoma de Santo Domingo and Pedro Henriquez Ureña. For twenty years Ana has taught in the Public Education System of the City of New York and is the author of two publications of poetry: *Del sentir y del ser* (2010) and *Despierten las aves* (2012).

Ana Isabel Saillant Valerio nació en Santiago de los Caballeros (República Dominicana). Emigró a los Estados Unidos en 1973, donde obtuvo una Maestría en Educación Bilingüe y una Licenciatura en Educación Elemental en The City College of New York. Realizó estudios en la Universidad Autónoma de Santo Domingo y Pedro Henriquez Ureña. Es la autora de *Del sentir y del ser* (2010) y *Despierten Las Aves* (2012). Ana Isabel es una profesora con 20 años de servicio en el sistema educativo público de la ciudad de New York en El Bronx.

CARTAS DE ESTACIONES

Rebusco en la lejanía
y trato de encontrar mensajes en la poesía,
encuentro sonidos de voces
en el teclado del ayer,
cartas de estaciones
donde la inocencia se alía a la pasión,
es hora de la flor
donde las sábanas son mojadas,
cartas de estaciones en el lenguaje de un día
que jamás serían expresadas
en el lenguaje invernal…
He encontrado sonido de poesía
en el tiempo desnudo.
Denuncia de pasión y pureza
Cartas de estaciones…
Te leo y te vuelvo
y te leo
tratando de adivinar
tu lenguaje estacionario.

RUBÉN MEDINA
[MÉXICO]

Rubén Medina (México)

Rubén Medina was born in Mexico City in 1955. He is a poet, translator, academic, editor, and one of the founders of Infrarrealism whose members include Mario Santiago Papasquiaro, Roberto Bolaño, Bruno Montané Krebs, Mara Larrosa, José Peguero, Cuauhtémoc Méndez, among others. He has lived in the US since 1978. In poetry he has published *Báilame este viento, Mariana* (1980), *"Amor de lejos...Fools' Love* (Arte Publico Press,1986), *Nomadic Nation / Nación nómada* (2010), and poems in numerous anthologies in the US, Mexico, Latin America and Spain. In the area of research he has published: *Autor, autoridad y autorización: escritura y poética de Octavio Paz* (Colegio de México, 1999), and *Genealogías del presente y del pasado: Literatura y cine meXicanos* (Latinoamericana, 2010). In collaboration with John Burns he translated a major anthology of Beat poetry into Spanish: *Una pandilla de salvajes improvisando a las puertas del infierno* (Aldus, 2012). Recently he edited *Perros habitados por las voces del desierto. Poesía infrarrealista entre dos siglos (Aldus, 2014)*. He received the NEA award fellowship in poetry in 1981. Since 1991 he has taught at UW-Madison, where he specializes in Mexican and Chicano/a literature and culture, intellectual history, film studies, and Mexican migration to the United States.

Rubén Medina nació en México, D.F. en 1955. Es un poeta, traductor, académico, editor, y uno de los fundadores del infrarrealismo, cuyos miembros incluyen Mario Santiago Papasquiaro, Roberto Bolaño, Bruno Montané Krebs, Mara Larrosa, José Peguero, Cuauhtémoc Méndez, entre otros. Ha vivido en Estados Unidos desde 1978. En poesía ha publicado: *Báila-*

me este viento, Mariana (1980), *"Amor de lejos...Fools' Love* (Arte Publico Press,1986), *Nomadic Nation / Nación nómada* (2010), así como poemas en varias antologías en Estados Unidos, México, Latinoamérica y España. En la investigación académica ha publicado: *Autor, autoridad y autorización: escritura y poética de Octavio Paz* (Colegio de México, 1999), y *Genealogías del presente y del pasado: Literatura y cine meXicanos* (Latinoamericana, 2010). En colaboración con John Burns publicó una extensa antología de poesía Beat en forma bilingüe, *Una pandilla de salvajes improvisando a las puertas del infierno* (Aldus, 2012). Recientemente editó en México, *Perros habitados por las voces del desierto. Poesía infrarrealista entre dos siglos* (Aldus, 2014). Ha recibido varios premios en poesía, incluyendo el NEA award in 1981. Since 1991 he teaches at the University of Wisconsin-Madison, donde se especializa en literatura y cultura mexicana y chicana, historia intelectual, estudios de cine, y migración mexicana a Estados Unidos.

BROWN BUFFALO

No te pude dar el Distrito Federal,
con sus azoteas insomnes,
sus catástrofes naturales y sociales,
sus calles repletas de historias anónimas
y conocimientos que no se aprenden
en las universidades,
sus saludos amorosos y agresivos.

Te traje, en cambio, por San Diego,
Oaxaca, San Francisco, Guanajuato,
Madison, Puerto Escondido, Tijuana,
mientras buscaba empleos
y espectáculos callejeros
en ciudades que ya nunca serían
como las de mi infancia y adolescencia.

Creciste por las carreteras,
en un triángulo por el que obstinadamente
uníamos a California, el Medio Oeste
y la altiplanicie mexicana. Y

en el camino devorabas libros,
tus manos dejaban de ser torpes,
escribías tus primeros poemas
y tu mirada fue descubriendo
lo que hay detrás del horizonte.

No te pude dar el Distrito Federal,
pero tú sabiamente escogiste otra metrópoli,
otra arena movediza,
acorde a tu propio pulso.
Y allí estás: Brown Buffalo
con Nueva York a tus pies
más que sobre tus hombros.

Siempre asumí que era
natural que los hijos
dejarían la casa y la familia
a los 18 años
como lo hice a esa misma edad.
Con los años ya no pienso igual.
Entre la libertad, la resignación y el egoísmo
se nos va la vida.

No te pude dar el Distrito Federal,
mi inquieto y joven búfalo:
por ahora tú escogiste Nueva York.

De *Ciudades de otros*

BROWN BUFFALO

I couldn't give you Mexico City
With its sleepless flat roofs,
Its natural and social catastrophes,
Its streets full of anonymous stories
And knowledge one does not learn
At universities,
And its aggressive and affectionate greetings.

Instead, I brought you San Diego, Oaxaca,
San Francisco, Guanajuato, Madison,
Puerto Escondido,Tijuana, Minnesota
While I searched jobs
And street gatherings
In cities that would never be like those
Of my childhood and adolescence.

You grew up on the highways,
Following a triangle that stubbornly
Connected California, the Midwest
And the Mexican tableland.

On the road you learned to read books,
Your hands stooped being clumsy,
You wrote your first poems,
And your eyes kept discovering
What was behind the mountains.

I couldn't give you Mexico City
But you intelligently chose another metropolis,
Another quicksand
In tune with your own pulse.
And there you are: Brown Buffalo
With New York City at your feet
Rather than over your shoulders.

I always assumed that at eighteen
Sons or daughters
should leave the house and family
as I did at that same age.
With the passing of years I have changed
My mind.
Between freedom, resignation and selfishness
Life passes on.

I couldn't give you Mexico City,
My young, unrestful, brown buffalo,
You chose New York for now.

TONIA LEÓN
[USA]

Tonia León was born in Brooklyn and reborn in Mexico. She has published poetry and prose in English and Spanish in the USA, Mexico, Colombia and Japan. Her first poetry collection entitled *My Beloved Chaos*, published in 2013, includes poems in English and Spanish. She also enjoys translating poetry from Spanish into English.

Tonia León cuenta que nació en Brooklyn y renació en México. Ha publicado poesía y prosa en inglés y en español en los E.U., México, Colombia y Japón. Su primer poemario *My Beloved Chaos* que se publicó en 2013 contiene poemas en inglés y español. También le encanta traducir poesía del español al inglés.

HOW TO LOVE A POET

Speak up in a whisper,
rush slowly to where he is,
consider carefully the words
which tumble from your mouth,
let your eyes smile at him tenderly
pulling apart the curtain of moments
to reveal the sweetest infinity,
rein in the poetry galloping through your blood,
if you dare to touch his hand
you'll both be instantly consumed
by an impossible frozen tropical Kiss.

COMO AMAR A UN POETA

Háblale fuerte en un murmullo
apúrate lentamente adónde él se encuentre
medita bien tus palabras
que quieren caer de tu boca
deja que tus ojos le sonrían con ternura
abriendo las cortinas de momentos
para revelar un dulce infinito.
frena la poesía
que corre por tu sangre
si te atreves a tocarle la mano
los dos estarán consumidos
por un imposible beso tropical en febrero.

FÉLIX GARCÍA
[R. DOMINICANA]

Félix García (R. Dominicana)

Félix García was born in San Francisco de Macoris, Dominican Republic. Poet, Teacher and Cultural Activist. Holds a BA in Education of the Universidad Autónoma de Santo Domingo. Founder and Coordinator of the Literary Workshop "Búsqueda" in Santo Domingo. He has resided in New York for many years. Co-editor of the Literary Magazine "Trazarte". He has several collections of Poetry: 04 *Todavia Queda*, 2001, 02 *Los soles del Ex*, unpublished, 2000, *Pasajero*, poetry-unpublished, 1997, *Tamor*, Poemas, 1994, *Mis Trece Cuerdos*, unpublished stories, 1990 y *Abril soneteando Un canto, 1986.*

Félix García nació en San Francisco de Macoris, Republica Dominicana. Poeta, maestro y gestor cultural. Licenciado en Educación, mención Filosofía y Letras de la Universidad Autónoma de Santo Domingo. Fundo y coordino el Taller literario *Búsqueda* en Santo Domingo. Reside en Nueva York hace nueve anos. Co-editor de la revista literaria Trazarte. Tiene varias colecciones de poesía: 04 *Todavía Queda*, 2001, 02 *Los soles del Ex*, inédito, 2000, *Pasajero*, poemas-inéditos, 1997, *Tamor*, Poemas, 1994, *Mis Trece Cuerdos*, cuentos inéditos, 1990 y *Abril soneteando Un canto, 1986.*

Magritte es otro sol que se revela o se enraíza desde trece corrientes
una gota que cae.
El prisma se solventa
y el sostén de la viga
se siembra tan profundo
como esa catarata de sol que es su desvelo

Magritte un Semí reencarnado colándose en el cubo del eco
repite la postura, no es postración, recita la llovizna
los réquiems de los mimos desde ahí.
Más, la voz imparable descubre
lo colado hacia el eco:
un follaje de piedras
abriendo tu rastro en medio día
un Semí como oruga
un collage entre grietas

CLARIBEL DÍAZ
[R. DOMINICANA]

Claribel Díaz is a poet and essayist born in Santo Domingo (Dominican Republic, 1963) She attended the Universidad Autónoma de Santo Domingo where she studied Psychology and Education (1989). She also earned a *Master's degree in Social Work* at *New York University –NYU-*. In 1989, she joined the César Vallejo literary workshop. Currently, Claribel works as psychotherapist at a mental health center in New York City where she has resided since 1996. She has published, among others, *Consideraciones psicodinámicas acerca de la delincuencia*, (Hermeneias del Psicoanálisis Editorial, 1987) and the poetry collections *Ser del Silencio/Being of Silence*, (Essential Icon Press, 2003) and *Órbita de la Inquietud*, (Obsidiana *Press*, 2010).

Claribel Díaz es una poeta y ensayista nacida en la ciudad de Santo domingo, R. D en 1963. Egresada de la Facultad de Humanidades de la Universidad Autónoma de Santo Domingo –UASD- en la que obtuvo los títulos de Licenciatura en Psicología en 1989 y Profesorado en Letras en 1993. Posee además el título de *Master in Social Work* de la *New York University –NYU-*. Miembro del Taller Literario César Vallejo desde el 1989. Actualmente, trabaja como Psicoterapeuta en un Centro de Salud Mental de la Ciudad de Nueva York en donde reside desde el 1996. Ha publicado, entre otros escritos, el opúsculo: *Consideraciones psicodinámicas acerca de la delincuencia*, (Hermeneias del Psicoanálisis Editorial, 1987) ylos libros de poesía: *Ser del Silencio/Being of Silence*, (Essential Icon Press, 2003) y *Órbita de la Inquietud*, (Obsidiana *Press*, 2010).

IMPOSIBILIDAD DE LOS DÍAS

Todo lo que me circunda está lejos
como el eco de tantas voces que se apagan.

Rueda el tiempo por la calle
y se lastiman sus rodillas en la acera.
Rebelándose,
con los pies en alto me requiere.
Me interpela,
escupiendo sobre la orfandad de mi rostro,
sobre la desolación de mi frente:
¿Adónde vas cuando la tarde ya cansada,
bebe su anaranjado líquido de cristal entre las sombras
y se desvanece?
¿A quién esperas en este rincón de la noche
queriendo atrapar por siempre el olor del recuerdo?
¿Quién te dijo que el día se hizo para guiar andanzas
de seres absortos por el desvelo?

Entonces vuelvo, interrumpida,
a dibujar la postración de las hojas,
a amordazar el ímpetu de los pájaros
y a auscultar en la prisa la perennidad con que
transcurre la espera.

Te presiento siempre en la inquietud,
en la imposibilidad de los días,
en la decrepitud del instante.

Te vas dejándome extraviada.
Regresas y me encuentro a la deriva,
descalza sobre los mismos pasos.

SERGIO ANDRUCCIOLI
[ARGENTINA]

Sergio Andruccioli was born in Buenos Aires (Argentina). In 1990 he moved to Miami. He attended Miami-Dade Community College and Florida International University (FIU) earning two BAs in English and Spanish. He also received an MA in Hispanic American Literature from FIU. Sergio has lived in New York since 2007. He has been a student in the doctoral program in Hispanic Languages and Literature at The Gradute Center (CUNY). He wrote for the literary section of Hora Hispana-Daily News. Sergio has taught ESL, Spanish and Literature at several institutions. Currently, he is teaching at Borough of Manhattan Community College (BMCC) and John Jay College. His first poetry collection will be published this fall.

Sergio Andruccioli nació en Buenos Aires, Argentina. En 1990 se radicó en Miami. Estudió en Miami-Dade Community College y en Florida International University (FIU), de donde egresó con una doble Licenciatura en literaturas inglesa y española y una Maestría en literatura hispánica. Desde el 2007 reside en Nueva York. Ha estudiado en el programa de doctorado en Lengua y Literaturas Hispánicas en el Centro de Graduados de la Universidad de la Ciudad de Nueva York (CUNY). Fue colaborador en la sección literaria de Hora Hispana-Daily News. Ha enseñado inglés como segundo idioma, lengua y literaturas. Actualmente es profesor de lengua y literatura en Borough of Manhattan Community College y en John Jay College de la ciudad de Nueva York. Su primera colección de poemas se publicará en el otoño de 2014.

NADIE

No duerme nadie
Nadie   nadie
Me inclino en silencio sobre mis dudas
No duermen ellas ni el hechizo que las engendra.
Mi poeta dijo que no duerme nadie
No se puede dormir
Con tanta sensibilidad a cuestas
No se puede dormir
Mientras todo esto sucede.
¡Cuánta razón tienes Federico!
No duerme nadie.

TOMÁS MODESTO GALÁN
[R. DOMINICANA]

Tomás Modesto Galán. Dominican writer, professor and cultural activist, who has lived in New York since 1986. He holds a Master's degree from Universidad Autonoma de Santo Domingo. Galan has been a professor of Spanish and others courses at the U.A.S.D. In New York, he works at CUNY and Pace University. Currently, he teaches at York College. He is the Cultural Coordinator of the Latino-American Book Festival *Libro Abierto.* Some of his works have appeared in several anthologies: *Voces de Ultramar, Viajeros del Rocío, Tertuliando,* and *Brújula & Compass* 28, de 1998. His book *Los Niños del Monte Edén* was translated into English by the poet Maria Bennett and edited by the Actor Water Krochmall and the poet Rhina Espaillat. He has published: Los Cuentos de Mount Hope (novel, 1995) and *Los niños del Monte Edén* (short stories, 1998), Cenizas del Viento (poetry, 1983), *¿Es popular la poesía de Juan Antonio Alix?* (essay, 1987), Diario de Caverna (poetry, 1988), Subway (poetry, 2008). His most recent publication is *Los cuentos de Mount Hope,* 2nd ed. (2014). He writes novels, essays, critiques, poetry and has an unpublished memoir.

Tomás Modesto Galán. Escritor dominicano que reside en Nueva York, desde el 1986. Tiene Maestría de la Universidad de Santo Domingo. Ha sido profesor de Español y de otras asignaturas en la U.A.S.D. En Nueva York labora en The City University of New York (CUNY) y en Pace University. Actualmente en York College. Es coordinador cultural y Comisionado de la Feria Literaria Latinoamericana *Libro Abierto.* Sus primeros escritos aparecieron publicados en los suplementos literarios de los periódicos: *La Noticia, Hoy* y en *Artes y Letras (Rep. Dom.). Textos suyos han aparecido en las antologías: Voces de Ultramar, Viajeros del Rocío, Tertuliando* y en *Brújula & Compass* 28, de 1998. Su libro *Los Niños del Monte Edén* fue traducido al inglés por la poeta Maria Bennett y editado por el actor Water Krochmall y la poeta Rhina Espaillat. Entre sus obras más importantes se encuentran: *Los Cuentos de Mount Hope* (novela, 1995) y *Los niños del Monte Edén* (cuentos, 1998). Entre sus obras publicadas sobresalen: *Cenizas del Viento* (poesía, 1983), *¿Es popular la poesía de Juan Antonio Alix?* (ensayo, 1987), y *Diario de Caverna* (poesía, 1988), *Subway* (poesía, 2008). Su mas reciente publicación es *Los cuentos de Mount Hope* (2014). Su obra que comprende novelas, ensayos, critica, poesía y memoria aun permanece inédita.

¿POR QUÉ AMENAZO DESCENDER HACIA MI PROPIA SOMBRA?

¿De qué mesías sufro? Nadie puede curar este delirio sacerdotal, ni sepultar un Mahoma alegre en el horizonte denunciado. Arriban Yorubas y Mandelas del gran sur africano. Marchamos de nuevo hacia el pretérito, en busca de un Llanero solitario negro que nunca ha estado en Harlem. Para sospecha, ahí está el tan necesario George Washington. Hay un puente lleno de pavos congelados, muy lejos del nunca jamás, de los quizás almidonados o del lúgubre sí de un labor day parade. Las ganancias no se dividen en pedacitos amarrados con alas de murciélagos. Nunca vendrá un mayo de esperanzas tontas ni caricias tributarias de la narcocracia universal de las torres ¿Por qué me doy el lujo de morir tan lejos y vivir tan cerca?

GUIDO ERNESTO CABRERIZO BARRIENTOS [BOLIVIA]

Guido Ernesto Cabrerizo Barrientos (Cochabamba, Bolivia, 1958). He resides in New York City where he published his poetic work, *Guadalupe* (2010). This book brought him a lot of satisfaction. He also made incursions in the art of performance with "Versos interactivos", a play under the direction of Maria Consuelo Garcia. He is an active part of the Collective Poets in New York and a member of the editorial committee of the newspaper "Vecindad." His works are published for the Xlibrix, an editorial that is working on his next book *Andamios*.

Guido Ernesto Cabrerizo Barrientos (Cochabamba, Bolivia 1958). Actualmente reside en Nueva York, ciudad donde publicó su obra poética *Guadalupe* en el año 2010. Este libro le trajo grandes satisfacciones. Cabrerizo también incursionó en el arte del Performance con "Versos interactivos", obra dirigida por María Consuelo García. Es parte activa del Colectivo de Poetas en Nueva York y miembro del Comité Editorial del Periódico Vecindad. Sus obras son publicadas por Xlibrix, editorial que está trabajando en su próximo libro *Andamios*.

Estoy viajando en calles, trenes,
llego a estaciones colmadas de gente
que no espero, ni me esperan.
Estoy viajando en tinta, en tertulias,
en aplausos generosos, en recuerdos
dulces y tristes, en laberintos de libros
que leo, me embarco en la nave de mi infancia,
en la esquina de mis sueños entre estrellas y cometas,
subo a la nave de El Principito, viajo con él
para mejor entenderme y entender la vida,
él me lleva dulcemente a viajar a mi interior
y sigo viajando en mí.
Estoy viajando y me interno en la pintura
de Bayro, me paseo en sus colores antiguos
y frescos acompañado de su Amanda,
ella me transporta y percibo que nos asomamos al canto
melodioso e irresistible de sirenas, salgo entre
espejos, pandoras y prostíbulos con sabor a naranja,
me despiden en un carnaval de colores
payasos, saltimbanquis, hombres, mujeres
y entre ellas, La Dama Apenada.
Me desprendo en la pintura de Posada
que me lleva a separarme de mí mismo para entrar
a un mundo seductor y transformador.
Viajo por mis andamios.
Estoy viajando en largas jornadas en copas y meseros,
fiestas que no son las mías,
entre bailarinas, músicos, poetas, escritores y pintores,
en bufandas, collarines y carteras,
en el tic tac de un reloj blanco,
en rosas rojas y soy cada pétalo sin miedo a marchitarme...
pausa, silencio, siento que estoy viajando a ti, amor mío.

RICARDO ALBERTO MALDONADO
[PUERTO RICO]

Ricardo Alberto Maldonado (Puerto Rico) has been granted fellowships by the New York Foundation for the Arts and Queer/Arts/Mentorship. Ricardo works for the 92Y Unterberg Poetry Center. He was born and raised in Puerto Rico.

Ricardo Alberto Maldonado (Puerto Rico) ha sido seleccionado como becario por el New York Foundation for the Arts y Queer/Arts/Mentorship. Trabaja para el 92Y Unterberg Poetry Center. Nació y se crió en Puerto Rico.

AMERICA! AMERICA!

In interiors by night-light and by our own
        admission, we levitate.

It is our birthright. Suppose the cargo was brought
        for our welfare: a kind

of instruction toward ill, produce
        we could not afford.

An attempt to recover the economy
        of youth,

thoughts about the climate and the waste
        of our prose.

There were trees the storm had reserved,
        fathers unmannered at the effort.

Our theater confused the gods.

We observed the trees. We never knew the fluttering
        made them distinct.

CAMILLE RANKINE
[USA]

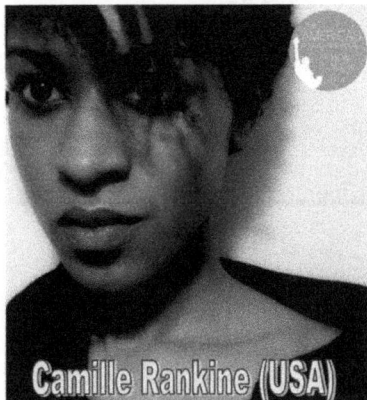

Camille Rankine's first book of poetry, *Incorrect Merciful Impulses,* is forthcoming from Copper Canyon Press. She is the author of the chapbook *Slow Dance with Trip Wire,* selected by Cornelius Eady for the Poetry Society of America's 2010 New York Chapbook Fellowship, and the recipient of a 2010 "Discovery"/ *Boston Review* Poetry Prize. Her poetry has appeared in *Atlas Review, American Poet, The Baffler, Boston Review, Denver Quarterly, Octopus Magazine, Paper Darts, Phantom Limb, A Public Space, Tin House,* and elsewhere. She is Assistant Director of the MFA Program in Creative Writing at Manhattanville College, Editorial Director of *The Manhattanville Review,* and lives in New York City.

El primer libro de Camille Rankine, *Incorrect Merciful Impulses,* será publicado por Copper Canyon Press. Es autora de la plaquette *Slow Dance with Trip Wire* que fue seleccionada por Cornelius Eady para recibir la beca de Poetry Society of America's 2010 New York Chapbook Fellowship y recibió el premio "Discovery" otorgado por *Boston Review* (2010). Sus poemas han aparecido en *Atlas Review, American Poet, The Baffler, Boston Review, Denver Quarterly, Octopus Magazine, Paper Darts, Phantom Limb, A Public Space, Tin House,* entre otros. Camille es Assistant Director en el porgrama de Maestría en Escritura Creativa de Manhattanville College y directora editorial de *Manhattanville Review.* Camille vive en Nueva York.

THE PROBLEM OF DEATH WITHIN LIFE

Given leave to speak, I shape my tongue
into a shovel and ask for more.
I should have told the truth, but
the truth is incomplete. I seek the missing
pieces and my eyes go lazy. It's a choice
I make that ruins me. I get off easy. I let myself go.
I hide the faces of the dying, wrap what remains
in lace and tuck it in the bottom drawer.

I'm sure I've pitied you
all wrong. I don't know how
it's done. I never learned.
I engulf with an affection from a chasm
in my gut, a sweet trap door, a heart-shaped hole,
a pretty well that threatens to swallow me up.

This is a brief malfunction. When you shift
out of the frame, the feeling shorts
and dissipates in sparks.
What a mess I've made of this
emotion. It's only endlessness
I've wanted. I can't fill my bowl, or yours.
I can't keep my fool mouth shut.

[first published in *Octopus Magazine,* Number 16, January 2014]

ANGELO VERGA
[USA]

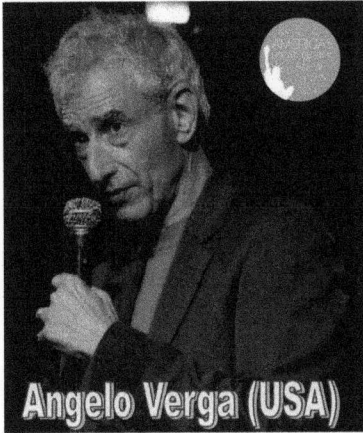

Angelo Verga (USA) is the author of six poetry collections. His poems have appeared *in Rattle, Manhattan Review, Massachusetts Review, New Orleans Poetry Forum, Blue Mesa Review, Saint Ann's Review, Paterson Literary Review, New York Quarterly, The Temple, Connecticut Poetry Review, Barrow Street, Heliotrope*, and numerous other journals. *A Hurricane Is* (Jane Street Press, 2003); *33 New York City Poems* (Booklyn, 2005); and *Praise for What Remains* (Three Rooms Press, 2010). He curates literary readings and other cultural events at the seminal Cornelia Street Cafe, & elsewhere. Saltonstall Foundation Poet in Residence (2001), Bronx Council on the Arts BRIO award winner (1999).

Angelo Verga (USA) es autor de seis volúmenes de poesía. Sus poemas han aparecido, entre otros, en: *in Rattle, Manhattan Review, Massachusetts Review, New Orleans Poetry Forum, Blue Mesa Review, Saint Ann's Review, Paterson Literary Review, New York Quarterly, The Temple, Connecticut Poetry Review, Barrow Street y Heliotrope*. Sus libros más recientes son *A Hurricane Is* (Jane Street Press, 2003); *33 New York City Poems* (Booklyn, 2005); y *Praise for What Remains* (Three Rooms Press, 2010). Angelo organiza lecturas y eventos literarios en lugares tan importantes como Cornelia Street Cafe. En 2001 fue poeta en residencia de Saltonstall Foundation y el 1999 recibió el premio BRIO del Concejo para las artes de El Bronx.

ELLIS ISLAND

High-ceilinged shower, white tiles two-thirds up its walls
And gaping drains to wallow dirty hair
High narrow slits to control the sun.
No way to look out, all day, as tedious as steerage
Unseen warships, sloops crisscrossing the gray bay
Massive wash basins and clanging sleep chambers
Men and women separated, different jails.
And strong blood wardens along parapet parade
14 desks summon butchered last names
Chalk marks: demerits for limping, talking to your self
Being with child, anarchist, unruly, or infirm.
You had to take $25 from your pocket
When $25 was 3 months pay
Sewing clothes, rolling cigars, blocking hats.
Deloused on foreign staircase,
"Kissing" posts, one for TB and whooping cough
Another for idiots, and seditious strangers.
Verga: the steel wall speaks my surname 13 times.
My father's mother, her girdle held her 6th month swell
Hidden, secret for 80 years, silent in a New World, till I say it.

ELLIS ISLAND

Regadera de techo alto, lozetas blancas dos terceras partes de sus techos
Y rejilla del desagüe para recoger pelo sucio
Altas estrechas rendijas para controlar la entrada del sol.
No hay manera de mirar hacia afuera, todo el día, tan tedioso como en bodega
Barcos de guerra no vistos, balandras entrecruzando la bahía gris
Palanganas enormes y ruidosas recámaras de dormir
Hombres y mujeres separados, diferentes celdas,
Y fuertes guardias rubios a lo largo de un desfile de parapeto
14 sillas citan apellidos descuartizados
Marcas de tiza: demérito por cojear, por hablar solo,
Estar con niño, anarquista, indomable, o endeble.

Usted tenía que sacar $25 de su bolsillo
Cuando $25 equivalía a 3 meses de sueldo
Cosiendo ropa, enrolando tabaco, moldeando sombreros.
Sin piojos en escalera extranjera
Postes de "besar", uno para tuberculosis y tos ferina
Otro para idiotas, y extranjeros sediciosos.
VERGA: la pared de metal dice mi nombre 13 veces.
La madre de mi padre, su faja la ocultó 6 meses hinchada
Secreto por 80 años, guardado, silenciado en un Nuevo Mundo, hasta que lo dije.

Traducido al español por Madeline Millán.

JUAN ANTONIO GONZÁLEZ FUENTES [ESPAÑA]

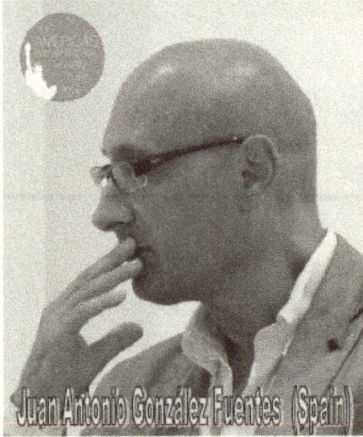

Juan Antonio González Fuentes (Santander, Spain, 1964). He studied Philosophy and Literature at Universidad de Cantabria. As poet, he has published *Además del final* (Endymión, 1998), *La luz todavía* (DVD, 2003) *Atlas de perplejidad* (Icaria, 2004), *La lengua ciega* (DVD, 2009) and *Monedas sueltas. Haikus 2009-2013* (Huerga & Fierro, 2014). He is the coeditor of *Espacio Hierro. Medio siglo de creación poética de José Hierro* (Fundación Botín-Universidad de Cantabria, 2001); *María Zambrano, la visión más transparente* (Trotta, 2004) and *José de Ciria y Escalante, prosas y poemas (1919-1924)* (Icaria, 2010), *La gracia irremediable. Álvaro Pombo, poéticas de un estilo* (Milrazones, 2013) and *Vicente Huidobro y Gerardo Diego en Vanguardia* (Ediciones La Bahía, 2014). His poetry has been included in anthologies such as *Campo abierto. Antología del poema en prosa en España (1990-2005)* (DVD, 2005), *Poetas en blanco y negro contemporáneos* (Abada, 2006) and *Littérature espagnole contemporaine* (Presses Universitaires de France, 2009).

Juan Antonio González Fuentes (Santander, España, 1964). Licenciado en Filosofía y Letras por la Universidad de Cantabria. Como poeta ha publicado *Además del final* (Endymión, 1998), *La luz todavía* (DVD, 2003) *Atlas de perplejidad* (Icaria, 2004), *La lengua ciega* (DVD, 2009) y *Monedas sueltas. Haikus 2009-2013* (Huerga & Fierro, 2014). Es coeditor de *Espacio Hierro. Medio siglo de creación poética de José Hierro* (Fundación Botín-Universidad de Cantabria, 2001); *María Zambrano, la visión más transparente* (Trotta, 2004) y *José de Ciria y Escalante, prosas y poemas (1919-1924)* (Icaria, 2010), *La gracia irremediable. Álvaro Pombo, poéticas de un estilo* (Milrazones, 2013) y *Vicente Huidobro y Gerardo Diego en Vanguardia* (Ediciones La Bahía, 2014). Su poesía ha sido incluida en antologías como *Campo abierto. Antología del poema en prosa en España (1990-2005)* (DVD, 2005), *Poetas en blanco y negro contemporáneos* (Abada, 2006) o *Littérature espagnole contemporaine* (Presses Universitaires de France, 2009).

PLAYA

Es en el aire de sí misma donde la ola intuye el signo del pie sobre la arena, ese hilo de fuerza que una y otra vez reclama ahondar en la espuma, escribir el propio ser en la dura piel de la roca. Con un salto la ola tantea el vacío, marca voraz la tierra envuelta en su propia hondura. La ola pesa y es tiempo y movimiento y desemboca en huida, en un bautismo sostenido por el fugaz destello de su predecible e incansable ruina. La ola se vuelve del revés, y busca la orilla como un río llegado de entre los muertos para ahogarnos en la falsa ceniza de sus notas falsas.

Y ahora que hablamos de la muerte, es en la playa donde la ola espera el anuncio inalterable de nuestro reino que llega con voz ahogada, con el mirar acuoso que busca su lenguaje arriba, en un cielo de silencio moteado por la sombra. Somos olas cuando llegan a la playa.

GREGORY CROSBY
[USA]

Gregory Crosby is the author of the chapbook *Spooky Action at a Distance* (2014, The Operating System); his poetry has appeared in numerous journals, including *Court Green, Epiphany, Copper Nickel, Leveler, Sink Review, Ping Pong, & Rattle.* In 2002, as a poetry consultant to the City of Las Vegas, he was instrumental in the creation of the Lewis Avenue Poets Bridge, a public art project in downtown Las Vegas. His dedicatory poem for the project, "The Long Shot," was subsequently reproduced in bronze and installed in the park, and was included in the 2008 anthology *Literary Nevada: Writings from the Silver State* (University of Nevada Press). He is co-editor of the online poetry journal *Lyre Lyre* and currently teaches creative writing at Lehman College, City University of New York.

Gregory Crosby es autor de la plaquette *Spooky Action at a Distance* (2014, The Operating System); sus poemas han aparecido en numerosas revistas literarias como *Court Green, Epiphany, Copper Nickel, Leveler, Sink Review, Ping Pong, & Rattle.* En 2002, como consultor en poesía para la ciudad de Las Vegas, colaboró en la creación del puente de los poetas en Lewis Avenue como parte de un proyecto en el centro de la ciudad. Su poema de dedicación al proyecto "The Long Shot" fue fundido en bronce e instalado en el parque. En 2008 fue incluido en la antología *Literary Nevada: Writings from the Silver State* (University of Nevada Press). Es coeditor de la revista virtual de poesía *Lyre Lyre* y en la actualidad enseña escritura creativa en Lehman College, City University of New York.

Gregory Crosby/ senormisterioso@gmail.com

A MIRACULOUS COCOON OF PIANOS

Every problem looks like a hammer when you're a key.
There must be more to this than merely crawling head first
from the wreck, through the soft cacophony of blanket forts
to the rebarbative rebar of buildings, collapsed. One day
the world comes crashing down around your ears. Take note.
An accordion wheezes while a lung makes love to a
broken rib. There must be more to all this than "Chopsticks."
Perhaps it's just not our forte, a big bang followed by
that little puff of "Smoke Gets in Your Eyes." Music is a
house with no roof, standing over the dream of a sinkhole,
where only the windows, the view, matters. Did I say *music*?
You know what I really meant: the chrysalis called tempo,
metronome in the dark. Whenever you're near, I hear
a sympathy, a cry from the very heart of noise.
A voice said, *Music saved my life*, & the voice was neither
wrong nor right. Hands claw the debris: finger exercises.
When the world lifts off your chest like a bully bored at last,
that's the silence of the recital hall, the hands hovering,
above it all, for a moment, in the astonished light.

www.ingramcontent.com/pod-product-compliance
Lightning Source LLC
Chambersburg PA
CBHW021229090426
42740CB00006B/445